IMAGES

John W. Tranter, Jr.

IMAGES

John W. Tranter, Jr.

Copyright © 1986 by TWO Communications, Inc.
Printed in the United States Of America
ISBN: 0-88368-183-8

Edited by David L. Young

DEDICATION

To my wife, Suzan, who simply believed.

Inquiries concerning seminars and personal ministry may be addressed to:

TWO Ministries, Inc.
P. O. Box 834
Wetumpka, Alabama 36092

CONTENTS

What would you do if you knew someone was trying to seduce your young son or daughter? Does it make your blood boil when you imagine an elderly woman being abused by unfeeling people who have no remorse for what they are doing? You are going to read about incredible manipulation in this book. These atrocities are not taking place in a distant land but right here. It's happening to your family, your children, your grandparents, your friends—and to *you*.

Chapter 1

THREATENING SKIES

Case #1

Billy looked like any normal twelve-year old. He carried the hopes and dreams of his parents. Yet there was a difference: Billy was an alcoholic and a thief. He had to be locked in his room at night to keep him off the streets.

Case #2

The Smith family was well-respected in the community. They had many prominent friends, were comfortable financially, attended church faithfully, and were even Bible teachers; yet an unseen force was at work that brought catastrophic results. One of their children became a homosexual, and another experienced a nervous breakdown. The father lost his job, and soon the family that had been a pillar in the community lay in shambles.

Case #3

The affluent upper-class parents were shocked by

the crime their son had committed. The film, *Taxi Driver,* had become a distorted reality for young John Hinckley, who attempted to kill the President of the United States in order to enhance the fantasy relationship he had created with actress Jodie Foster.

These three cases, along with many others, led to the writing of this book. What do they have in common? Many parents, troubled by changes in their children, were coming to us in desperation, wanting to know why their children were behaving illogically. Often the young person's behavior was out of line with the way he or she had been raised. Many of the kids were becoming wild and rebellious, even criminal. What were the forces at work capable of destroying families and leaving relationships shattered? What was it that left these parents in such a bewildered state?

Know this—there *are* answers! As you read this book, the author requests that you commit to do two things: First, if a section seems obscure, don't give up. The mystery will be cleared as the entire picture begins to unfold. Secondly, pray for understanding. Without the Holy Spirit's guidance, we will fall short, for "He will guide [us] into all truth" (John 16:13).

You are being manipulated. That may sound like a strong statement, perhaps peculiar, but it is true nonetheless. In fact, glaring examples of manipulation occur all around us. You and your family are being programmed, subliminally manipulated to become something you do not want to be. When you begin to realize what is happening, an indignation will begin to rise within you. But let's not get too far ahead. Perhaps we should go back to where the idea for this book first began.

The Enemy's Camp

I first became aware of the hidden forces at work within our nation while attending graduate school. Clues were all around, but no one seemed to be particularly alarmed. Jerry Falwell's name would come up frequently. In fact, it was used as one of the most popular objects of ridicule and contempt among professors and students. The Moral Majority was frequently likened to the Nazi Party or the KKK, and Falwell was portrayed as the USA's own Ayatollah. Scorn spewed from the "pulpits" of the classrooms as Reagan, fundamentalist Christians, pro-life groups, and conservatives in general were made to look like buffoons.

Perhaps most alarming was the nature of the classes. These were not political or philosophical courses. They were supposed to be instructional sessions for journalism students. Think about that. Students were not just being trained in how to report the news, they were being indoctrinated in a system of total world outlook. Professors dogmatically taught that the enemies of the press consisted of religious and conservative groups. An entire graduate body was being educated and armed to fight these "dangerous elements." It is one thing to hear a preacher speak from the pulpit about humanists distorting the truth in the mass media but quite another to actually sit in on the training of these future media powerbrokers.

You might think that such a venemous attack day in and day out would alert anyone that something was out of kilter in the system. I'd *like* to say that these clues instantly lit up great revelations as I began studying behind-the-scene truths in mass media. Unfortunately, this was not the case. Like many others, I had serious doubts about the idea of a conspiracy. This, combined with indifference and self-interest, led to what most people are doing: nothing. It took an incident in the classroom to shake me to my senses—something even I couldn't miss.

It began innocently enough. After hearing many horrible things about Jerry Falwell and the Moral Majority, I decided to devote an entire course to investigate the organization and the media's coverage of it. In graduate school, courses cover a wide range of topics. Often the choice of study is left to the student. I chose a subject that was obviously interesting to almost the entire school—the "Media and the Moral Majority."

My findings were interesting but hardly out of the ordinary. The press consistently reported Jerry Falwell and the Moral Majority in negative terms. This caused no surprise. If a group is thought to be bad, it should be reported as bad. When my findings were presented before the class and the professor, only part of the research caused unrest.

The trouble spot was the section dealing with the relatively small group who decide what goes into newspapers, what gets on television, and what is heard on the radio. This part analyzed what this group of media elite actually felt about key issues, such as homosexuality and abortion.

When this part of the research was presented, the response was immediate and violent. The professor actually interrupted my report to declare emphatically that the facts were false. The students began to audibly grumble as the picture began to unfold. The media elite clearly had their minds made up about certain issues and were reporting what they wanted the public to believe, not necessarily what had taken place. It was this uncovering of the true nature and intentions of those controlling the mass media that brought such a violent reaction. A sensitive nerve had been hit—an area these journalism students and professors could not face.

This incident woke me up. There was something hidden that those controlling the mass media did not want out. This book is dedicated to exposing that hidden truth.

Chapter 2

END-TIME POWERBROKERS

Have you ever wondered where your favorite prime-time television program comes from? How does the program get on the screen as you see it? Most people never really consider how a television program is created. If we are to understand how the media is manipulating us, we must look at who is pulling the strings.

In television, a producer creates the show. He forms the content, develops characters, and ultimately directs the script and dialogue. It takes many talented people to get a program on the air, but the producer takes the helm of the ship and directs its course.

For example, a producer may imagine a new program that features a single father with three young sons. He imagines the setting as a white, middle-class neighborhood. This should appeal to his targeted audience (middle America). For added interplay, he decides to give the show a grumpy but lovable uncle who takes care of the kitchen and a big dog who gets into trouble. People should be able to identify with that. The producer believes in traditional family values so the father is widowed not divorced. This same father is pictured as wise, caring, sensitive, and devoted to his family. He is always written into the program as very effective in handling the boys' problems.

The boys, on the other hand, are created to be clean-cut, respectable, and without any real evil in their hearts. Have you recognized the format? It should sound like the once-popular show, *My Three Sons*.

Are you getting the picture? Television shows do not just appear on the screen. They are creations of intelligent people with dreams, feelings, shortcomings, opinions, and many motives—just like you. To illustrate, let's look at a simple example.

Early in my career, a children's ministry wanted to put together a TV show to reach the nation's young people. I was hired to produce the program. The first question I asked was, "What are we trying to do?" The objective was "to reach kids with the Christian message and teach them morals, work-ethics, manners, how to be good citizens, respect for authority, etc." In essence, the goal was to help make good, Christian kids.

The second question was, "How do we intend to accomplish the objective (teaching the children)?" This led to some confusion on the ministry's part since, like most people, they had never really considered this question. The organization's intention was to have one person teach the children from the screen, like a televised Sunday school class. This spelled disaster. To compete with today's sophisticated children's programs, more was needed than just the infamous "talking head."

After much thought and analysis, we decided to create certain characters who would get the message across by example. Simply stated, we wanted to bypass the drudgery of "instruction" and teach the desired lesson through entertainment. This was done by sending messages that children were not even aware of.

First, we developed characters. The host of the program, who would have been the teacher, became a character designed to represent Christianity. Puppets were given distinct personalities. One represented the child who hung in the balance—not bad, yet easily influenced by others. A different puppet represented the kid who always seemed to be in trouble. He was rebellious, impetuous, and quick to speak and lead others into trouble. Finally, at the opposite end, we developed a character to represent evil and temptation.

After the characters were developed to represent a type of person, we created situations in which these characters would interact. Crisis and conflict faced the puppets (kids). One puppet led the others down the wrong path despite the wise counsel of the host. Every program would then show the consequences of following this evil character. The host always ended up right, the puppets saw their error, and truth triumphed in the end. Evil was always shown to be foolish. Good was the smart way to go.

Every episode had a strong message. We didn't appear on the screen and say, "Kids, be good. What the Bible says is true. Don't follow what others tell you. Do what is right. Respect your elders, etc." Instead, characters represented personalities, and we wrote in "reality" by the way each show turned out. The messages were subliminally put into the minds of children through roles and examples.

Now that you've read how producers use shows to get messages across, turn your attention to *your* favorite prime-time program. Could you be the target of the same type of hidden messages, directed by someone without your benefit in mind?

M*A*S*H

After realizing the way television programs are really made, you can begin to see subtle messages written into the scripts. Take a look at a program that almost everyone is familiar with, *MASH*. Are there hidden messages in *MASH?* This is an important question since it is one of the most popular (and therefore powerful) programs of all time.[1] Remember, if you will, the original television characters.

Hawkeye was the lovable hero of the show. Have you ever thought about what Hawkeye stood for? What was he like? We could begin with the liquor still. The "swamp" was constantly the scene of heavy drinking. Next to drinking, Hawk's favorite activity was probably illicit sex. He was constantly trying to get the nurses to go to bed with him. He was also a heavy gambler. What else? He was rebellious—very rebellious against authority. Remember the generals he told off and the persistent downgrading of the entire purpose of the war? He disregarded the orders of the camp commander, was unshaven, scorned military dress, and hated discipline. Hawkeye was not a religious man. He seldom attended worship services; and if he did, it was not for the right reasons.

What was Hawkeye, then? He was the humanist's ideal personified. *Humanism* is the religion that makes man the center of the universe. Man has the responsibility and the ability to solve all his problems. God is a myth. Everything is relative. Morals are not absolute. Traditional values are outdated and meaningless, put forward by ignorant men. In short, if a humanist wanted to get this warped message into the minds of our youth, Hawkeye would be the perfect creation for millions to idolize.

Next, let's look at the stooge of the show—the man nobody liked—Frank Burns. Whatever Frank represented, it wasn't very popular in the producer's eyes because he made this character the lowest of vile and despicable creatures. Who was Frank, then? He was supposed to represent the traditional moral, church-going, family man. His Bible was brought out on several occasions. Pictured as the worst kind of bigot, he cheated on his wife and back-stabbed for

18

promotions. Frank was inadequate professionally and intellectually. He represents us, brothers and sisters in Christ. We are Frank Burns. How do you feel about your favorite TV show now? Wait, there's more.

If *MASH* promoted rebellion against authority, then look at those characters who represented it. How about Henry Blake? Remember the fumbling, inept company commander who wore a ridiculous fishing hat? He was our example of authority. But when the establishment was to be particularly torn apart, a special general was written into the script. Everything from blood-thirsty bigots to sex-crazed phonies came into the camp in all the decorations of famous generals.

Major Margaret Hulahan was another original character made to look ridiculous. She was under the heel of the same generals and establishment that Hawkeye constantly put down. Later in the show's life, "Hot Lips" was divorced and became liberated from the domain and oppression of the male-dominated establishment. She then fit in with Hawkeye's "inner circle" and became an accepted character.

What about Father Mulcahey? He gave us a glimpse of what the producer approves in religion. The Father was kind and likeable but extremely weak in evangelizing the camp. In fact, Mulcahey was the one who seemed to be "converted." He drank, gambled, and was given to fits of rage, yet he always came through as a warmhearted but naive do-gooder. The message is that a watered-down social gospel is okay, but forget that serious conversion, heaven-and-hell talk.

The man who really knew the answer to life was an atheistic psychiatrist. Sidney, the "priest" of secular humanism, knew just how to deal with the problems of the camp personnel. In the last episode of *MASH*, this man of science rescued Hawkeye from the psychological prison in which he had been trapped. The message: an atheistic, humanistic view of life is reality.

To recap, the hero of *MASH* was a humanist. The traditionally moral men and women were shown to be misinformed hypocrites. The social gospel was made to look good, and life's answers were found in the secular social sciences.

Seeds have now been planted into the subconscious minds of millions of avid viewers. Drinking, gambling, rebellion, promiscuity, and scepticism were hidden under the cloud of entertainment. Young viewers were not on guard to the constant barrage of evil messages.

An open door is given into the hearts and minds of our children as they sit for hours each week soaking in a humanistic "sermon." Many people watch *MASH* two or three times a day in reruns and syndication. Compare this incredible amount of time under the influence of humanism to the one hour per week of church that most kids must "endure." They often find church boring, and their conscious guards are evidently up as we see them drawing or talking to their friends during service. Parents, do you wonder why your child rejects your values and instead pursues the teachings of their heros?

Perhaps this breakdown of the very popular program has left you with doubts. You think, "Could it be true? Could there really be an effort to change the way my child views the world?"

For the doubters still among you, this fact should prove interesting: The screenplay for the original movie, *MASH,* was written by Ring Lardner, Jr., who served time in prison for communist activities in the United States.[2]

All In The Family

Once the key to understanding messages in the media is discovered, anyone can see the blatant use of programs to influence society. Another popular program was *All In The Family.* The main character, Archie Bunker, was a composite of white, lower-middle class, conservative men.

The producer of this program evidently intended to hold up traditional America with all its values to public ridicule and scorn. Bunker looked like an idiot. Every detail of the family atmosphere was designed to resemble your own home. What changed was how "reality" was written into the script. Remember, after characters are created, the message must be implanted by how the characters react and how conflict is resolved. In this case, Archie was ignorant and bigoted; simply put, he was a fool.

Then, of course, there was Edith. How many middle-aged women do you think identified with her position? This was the intent. Of course, the message inferred that Edith was even more of a fool than her husband. Women all across the country were told in episode after episode that the situation they were in at home was bondage. They were told that being a housewife was unfulfilling and that their husbands didn't really know what they were talking about.

The Bunkers' liberal, educated kids always seemed to know something their parents didn't. It was as though the older generation was living in some kind of sad delusion. They were more to be pitied and endured than respected and obeyed. Parents, have you detected this attitude coming from your children? Husbands, do you sense an outside influence drawing your family away? Where did those thoughts of inadequacy and unfulfillment originate? Who told you that you were being played for a fool? Television? Magazines? Who controls them?

Producer Norman Lear was the creative force behind *All In The Family*. According to *Forbes* magazine, he does not like to be challenged concerning his work.[3] A so-called "citizen group" founded by Lear, *People for the American Way,* has been described as perpetrating "an aggressive hate campaign against fundamentalist Christians."[4] No won-

22

der Lear and the Christian community are at odds. His works include *Maude, The Jeffersons, Mary Hartman: Mary Hartman, Good Times,* and *Hotel Baltimore* (featuring a homosexual relationship).[5]

Why are we so concerned about the message these powerbrokers are putting out? One reason is that television is accepted uncritically by millions of viewers. Over 145 million TV sets in the United States are being watched an average of 6.5 hours a day in each house. A child entering kindergarten is subjected to over thirty hours of television per week and over four hundred commercials. We spend the equivalent of *nine years* of our lives watching TV![6]

The influential power of television will be covered in greater detail in later chapters, but to bring out the severity of what these producers are accomplishing we must look at the power behind the medium.

TV is a universally shared experience that contributes to and *changes* our culture.[7] The set becomes a new member of the family, demanding attention and rearranging schedules. Many hours are spent watching the "most hypnotic and addictive medium in history."[8] Just how much do we subject ourselves to this bombardment? By the end of high school, a young adult has consumed *24,000 hours* of television, compared to only 12,000 in the classroom!

In a recent edition of the newspaper magazine, *Parade,* the headline read: "Does Hollywood Sell Drugs To Kids?" The feature cited several TV programs and movies that portray drug use in a favorable light.[9]

While we commend the magazine for this honest investigation into drug-related messages, we would like to ask where the investigations are for the rest of the garbage Hollywood is selling our kids? Yes, the drug message is affecting our society and is dangerous, but what about the free sex message? The alcohol message? Cigarettes? Homosexuality? Violence? The list goes on and on. *Everything* in our culture is influenced by a mass media that has forsaken traditional morality.

The list of television programs with anti-Christian messages is almost without end, and the list grows every day. A homosexual couple was made the focus of a so-called comedy show, *All Together Now.* One episode of *Hooker* portrayed a mad rapist/killer who left a Bible behind after abducting all his victims. The show, *Mork and Mindy,* frequently mocked television evangelists. The mini-series, *Space,* included a contemptible character who cheated, lied, and fooled around, although he was a minister.

Sarah was a program that depicted homosexuality, adultery, and fornication as the normal condition of the world. *That Was The Week That Was* devoted an entire comedy routine to the ridicule of the Christian Broadcasting Network and the Bible.[10]

Saturday Night Live almost always includes some

type of ridicule and contempt for Christianity, authority, and conservative viewers.

If you watch television, these descriptions should not surprise you. The preachers of secular humanism and sexual promiscuity have all but completely taken over the secular networks. Cable TV with its uncut movies and MTV sinks to new lows in morality and family programming.

We Christians must be aware of the nature of the media. Programs do not just have to appear on your screen. Behind every line and every character is a meaning. Preachers are ridiculed in prime-time shows, yet the very program itself is a sermon carefully prepared by the "preachers" of a new age. Don't be fooled by rhetoric. Television writers, producers, and advertisers know full-well the power they possess, and they are determined to use that power to alter you, your family, and your world.[11]

Chapter 3

MEDIA ELITE

It might be easy to think that the previous examples were isolated abuses, not representative of the opinions of the entire group of media gate-keepers and powerbrokers. After reading this chapter, you decide whether we have accurately described these people who play such a powerful role in shaping our lives.

Probably the most famous study of the media elite is the one conducted by S. Robert Lichter and Stanley Rothman of Columbia University.[1] These gentlemen conducted extensive interviews to discover the opinions, outlooks, morals, and goals of the media hierarchy. Their findings proved quite interesting.

The survey found "a substantial portion of the media elite . . . dissatisfied with the present social system"[2] and committed to the welfare state. Leading journalists emerged as "strong supporters of environmental protection, affirmative action, women's rights, homosexual rights, and sexual freedom in general." Ninety percent were pro-abortion, 85% uphold the right of homosexuals to teach in public schools, and only 15% strongly agree that extramarital affairs are immoral.

How would you like these people controlling the news you receive, the programs your children watch, the magazines that fill the stores, the radio airwaves, advertising, movies, and every other media outlet? The question is not how *would* you like it but rather how *do* you like it? These are the very people telling you what is real and what you should believe.

The report goes on to state that "a predominant characteristic of the media elite is its secular outlook." Eighty-six percent seldom or never attend religious services. "Thus, members of the media elite emerge as strong supporters of sexual freedom or permissiveness and as natural opponents of groups like the Moral Majority."[3]

Do you recall in the first chapter how we described a journalism professor's violent reaction to my report? This survey we are now citing is what hit such a sensitive nerve in this liberal professor and, indeed, the entire institution.

Unfortunately, at the time of the report, this survey had not appeared in the many evangelical and secular publications that have since featured it. At that point, it was just one student against the entire school—including the student body. The matter was dropped in the face of the apparent "expert" opinion that claimed it was in error. I took no small comfort in seeing the survey used dozens of times in subsequent articles. Sadly, an entire graduate class was misled by an opinionated professor who did not have his facts straight.

Don't be fooled by this same tactic. A favorite defense of the media is a vicious attack on whoever is exposing its deceits. In fact, don't be surprised if this book or its author is thoroughly torn apart by a furious media elite. And the next person on the hit-list will be you, once you become aware of what the media is doing to destroy your traditional values.

Another example of the true nature of those controlling the media is found in their voting habits. During the 1964 presidential election, 94% of the media elite voted for Johnson, while only 6% voted for Goldwater. In 1968, 87% voted for Humphrey. In 1972, 81% supported McGovern. Finally, in 1976, 81% voted for Carter. These voting records reveal a media way out of line with the general public. The democratic margin among elite journalists has been up to 50% greater than the public. The study states that these choices in selecting presidents "are consistent with the media elite's liberal views on a wide range of social and political issues."[4]

In another scholarly study, the media's coverage of the 1984 presidential campaign was analyzed. Maura Clancey and Michael J. Robinson flatly stated that "our quantitative evidence from all three networks states that correspondents in the general election campaign of 1984 did in almost every respect treat Reagan and Bush much more negatively than Mondale and Ferraro."[5] Ronald Reagan's press coverage on network television proved to be 90 percent negative. As incredible as this seems, George Bush topped this with absolutely *no* positive coverage! Of all the news that showed a slant, the Republican ticket received 95 percent negative coverage.

On the flip side, Mondale and Ferraro actually had more positive coverage than negative. The authors state, "Given what we know about the bad news bias of television, the fact that anyone, let alone any ticket, got more positive spin than negative is news indeed."[6] It must have taken incredible emotion to make the networks break down their own tradition of reporting bad news. Perhaps the audacity of the news departments in reporting with such an obvious slant has caused the recent dramatic downturn in the public's confidence in our country's press.

During this election, the press blamed Reagan for failures abroad, criticized him for injecting religion into politics, and made him personally responsible for the bombing of the marine base in Lebanon. In the reports that were supposed to be straight news, Reagan was criticized in a different way. There was "a near constant barrage of closures or interpretive remarks implying that something wasn't right with Reagan. He was hiding behind his security squad, he was cut off from the public, or he was manipulating symbols, or he was feeble-minded, or he was too old, or wasting taxpayer's money, or he was saying dumb things.''[7]

The top twenty most fully covered campaign issues were listed in order. Nine of the top ten were campaign issues that were negative news for Reagan/Bush. Neither Mondale's health problems with hypertension nor Ferraro's confusion between "first use" and "first strike" even made the list. Zaccaro/Ferrarogate came in way down at number twelve. With the liberal media elite deciding what was news, the *GOP* suffered five times the negative coverage compared to the democrats.

The most glaring example of news bias was the coverage of the 1984 campaign debates. The general agreement is that Mondale won the first debate, and the next two were close, favoring the President. This was not anywhere near the picture the network news painted. Twenty-seven times network reporters personally commented that Mondale won the first debate. These same reporters said absolutely nothing about Bush's victory in his debate with Ferraro. Reagan received more than thirteen times as much evening news comments for losing the first debate as he did for winning the second.

While the Vice-President was ignored concerning his debate performance, the networks pounced on his off-camera remark about "kicking a little—." Bush got more coverage for that statement than for any other area of the debate.

As these statistics show, the relatively small group that controls the media has an intense interest in using its power. In fact, it actually regards itself as the best group to direct society![8] Lichter and Rothman sum it up this way: "The pointed views of the national media elite are . . . the voice of a new leadership group that has arrived as a major force in American society. Cosmopolitan in the origins, liberal in their outlooks, *they are aware and protective of their collective influence.*"[9]

Let's face it, *MASH* and *All In The Family* are not isolated cases. The media is controlled by a powerful group who probably differ widely from you on most moral issues. These values come through in every program they produce and are then absorbed by you and your family, probably without your knowledge or consent. Yes, you *are* being manipulated!

Chapter 4

ADVERTISING

We have been concentrating on the messages hidden in the characters and story lines of various programs. Another area of concern is subliminal manipulation in advertising. How much of what we see contains an additional message directed toward our subconscious mind? The answer is very important since in a profit-motivated economic system almost all media is financed through advertising.[1] In fact, media's overriding purpose is to provide a platform for advertisers.[2]

With revenues exceeding $80 billion in 1984, the ad industry is doing its part to see that the multimedia is safe and sound. A thirty-second spot in prime-time now goes for $100,000 plus.[3] Magazines bring in billions of dollars each year from advertising revenue. It has reached the point where we are no longer customers of media, we are the *product* that media offers to advertisers (for a very handsome sum). Clearly, advertising is all around us, and advertising is here to stay.

If ads also contain subliminal messages, we cannot escape, for our culture is saturated with sell, sell. Take a moment to consider the vast network of advertising in our country—television, radio, newspapers, billboards, direct mail, store displays, catalogs, magazines, direct sales, telephone solicitation, and even low-flying aircraft at the beach.

Commercials begin, split, and end all programming on TV. It ends up totaling 22% of all broadcast time.[4] In the nine hours of media saturation that we endure daily, our senses (and subconscious) are bombarded by 500 ads and over 100,000 advertising words.[5] In this unrelenting attack, is there an effort to reach our subconscious mind? Here is how advertising stands up when investigated:

One of the most popular examples of hidden messages in advertising occurred in a movie theater and involved the instantaneous flashing of persuasive words during the film presentation. The machine, called a *tachistoscope*, projected the messages for only 1/300th of a second, far too quick for the conscious mind to perceive. Yet the audience responded in high percentages to the suggestions to eat popcorn and drink Coke.

If you are like most people, you think this type of subliminal seduction has been outlawed. The truth is that *no* law has been enacted to safeguard the American public from these professional manipulators.[6] There have been congressional investigations, but nothing has been carried through. Nothing, that is, except the expertise of these "salesmen."

Today machines do not flash messages intermittently but rather project a *steady* flow of messages just below the level of our awareness. These messages, which we can neither hear nor see, are perceived by our subconscious quite clearly.

Hal C. Becker, head of Behavioral Engineering Corporation, specializes in this type of subliminal communication, with machines currently operating in car dealers, supermarkets, and department stores. It is also available for home use. People are seeking out the technology to try and stop smoking or lose weight.[7] Picking the consumer apart has become high-tech with the latest psychophysiological devices (such as the oculometer, which tracks eye movements across the TV screen). We now have machines that test our eye, voice, body, and brain response to advertising stimuli.[8]

This technology is not used so marketers can present the logic of buying their brand over the competition. They are after the subconscious, for the consumer has proven again and again that most purchases are based on emotion, not logic.[9] Products are presented through the image created by advertising agencies. The consumer acts emotionally, unconsciously reacting to images associated with the product.

Many examples show how we buy images and feelings rather than products. We rationalize that we are buying soap for cleanliness, but actually the advertiser has promised us social acceptance and a feeling of refreshment. What to the rest of the world seems like extravagance in bathing habits has become to us the natural way of doing things. Ads continually seek to associate products with a "state of mind like wealth, status, virility, or good taste."[10]

In one of the ads for a weight-lifting machine called *DP,* there appeared what looked like a curved separation painted on the background. The weight machine sticks up between these two curves. As a man mounts the machine and begins to pump it up and down between the curves, female voices in the background can be heard to methodically repeat DP, DP, DP (deeper). The voices increase in tempo and intensity as the commercial reaches its climax with a sensuous young woman entering to hug the young man with apparent ecstasy. Does it take a Ph.D. to realize what the message is?

How about the Honda Scooter ad that is modeled after the successful music videos? The music is highlighted with night scenes of street people in the inner city. Punk rockers, a sax player on the corner, and all types of rough, tough, rebellious looking street-wise people are shown. What is the message to young people considering a scooter? The final shot is a man wearing sunglasses and a leather jacket looking at the camera and saying in his toughest voice, "Don't settle for walkin'." Kids are not told that scooters are fun, practical, or useful in any way. They are promised a macho image and then told bluntly not to take "no" for an answer. Don't settle for walkin'! Rebellion oozes through this image-laden commercial. What an appropriate name they have selected for their higher priced bike. They call it, *Rebel!*

For another example, consider the magazine ad that shows a young woman sitting by the edge of a pool with her legs spread, kicking up water. She laughs gleefully as a young man is positioned in the water with his head right in front of her lower body. Consider carefully the ad's copy. It tells us she is "alive with pleasure."

Remember, the object of these ads is to implant a message without having to deal with your perceptual defenses (morals, values, logic, etc.). Few people realize the assumptions marketers go on. Here are three you might find interesting: First, people don't know what they want. Second, if they do know, they can't be trusted to tell the truth. Lastly, they *cannot be counted on to behave rationally.*[11]

Isn't it ironic that the advertisements you thought were so stupid are really intelligently directed toward your subconscious with a hard-hitting message? This has been proven to affect your final behavior (i.e. choice of products). Somebody's laughing all the way to the bank.

Subliminal Artists

Several techniques are used to hide subliminal messages in advertising. One is to paint words, figures, or symbols over photographs, usually in the shadows or ripples of hair, ice, or complicated backgrounds. Another frequently used method leaves the message invisible to the naked eye but clearly visible to our subconscious. This involves writing the words on a photoengraving plate before processing the picture. The forbidden words bombard our hidden thoughts and motives without any conscious awareness on our part. You will find examples of these in the pictorial section of this book.

Another technique positions different characters and props in the scene to indicate shocking and sometimes offensive meanings.[12] A vodka ad that appeared in a national men's magazine used this technique. (See figure 2.) At first glance the ad appears quite innocent. The scene is a locker room/lounge at a golf course. A man is standing and presenting his friend with a plaque that has a broken golf club mounted on it. The message to our consious mind indicates a friendly, humorous get-together of golfing partners. They look as though they are having a good laugh over a club one of the characters has broken.

Closer examination reveals a hidden scene that would shock many men who read the magazine. The broken club on the plague is positioned to extend directly from the standing man's genital area. All the other men are looking at the obviously symbolic erection with their mouths open. One has his hand extended toward it. All are excited. In the background, two men are standing in compromising positions. One is caught in the act of urinating while the other is focusing his attention on his lower body.

Every man in the ad is therefore directed toward the genital area.

What our uninformed reader has encountered is not, as he thought, a gag gift among buddies. He has, in fact, witnessed blatant homosexuality. Several figures are painted into the surrounding area, including a nude female clearly seen in the shadows of the bottle of vodka.

Apparently, nothing is sacred or protected from the subliminal seducer's touch. Certain doll advertisements have had filthy words subliminally painted into the shaded areas of the doll's body.[13] Ads that exploit children are even finding their way into our everyday media world. Posing children seductively or in the nude has a terrible effect on the young *and* old. We have heard personal testimonies from men in a sex-offender's prison that reveal tragic consequences of our media's irresponsibility. Many of these men fed their perverted appetites with advertisements and films showing children in suggestive postures.

"Sex is being used to promote items as varied as cologne and traveler's checks."[14] This quote is from a 1980 issue of *Time* magazine and sums up the situation in the marketplace. As advertisers have known for years, sex sells. For example, a car commercial ends with a beautiful blonde leaning out the window of a car and saying in her most seductive voice, "Drive it home." You can bet she's not talking about any automobile. A traveler's check ad features a vacationing couple in a nude public bath.

One soap commercial reversed the male and female sexual identity of its characters to bring home an incredible message to everyone unfortunate enough to be watching. The man was shown as feminine, emotional, insecure, shrill, and looking to his wife for assurance. He is positioned in a window looking down on his wife (reversal of typical Romeo and Juliet). There are flowers at groin level. The wife, complete with button-down-collar and *flower shears,* assumes a dominate role in counseling the husband. A more blatant example is found in the now famous Gilbey's London Dry Gin ad. "Sex" is painted in the ice cubes of the featured drink. (See figure 1.)[15]

Most people are convinced that sex is being used to sell products. Anyone who watches TV or reads magazines is saturated with seduction and temptation.

An interesting addition to the sexual promises marketers are selling is the recent exploitation of spiritual needs—not crosses or Bibles but everlasting life! A recent TV commercial for a candy bar was narrated by an "angel" who encouraged us to buy the heavenly candy. We are told to "bite it and believe." A truck commercial featuring Noah and the ark ends with these interesting words: "Datsun Saves." Does it seem incredible to you that advertisers would stoop this low to sell us their products? Read on!

In 1971 an estimated $1 billion was wasted on deception and quackery.[16] Congressional hearings have found that most breakfast foods are nutritionally valueless and 15% of the over-the-counter drugs sold are absolutely useless.[17] Women currently wear furs without any idea of what they really are. What would you think of a fur called Alaskan Sable? It is really dyed skunk! Australian Seal is really dyed rabbit; Blue Japanese Wolf is dyed goat; Black Pioret Fox is dyed dog; and Russian Black Marten is really dyed opposum.[18]

Here are a few more examples of deceptive slogans: "99 and 44/100 percent pure." (Pure what?) "There's nothing like it!" (Maybe that's a good thing, too!)

"Our brand gives you a whiter wash!" (Than what?)

Here are two statements that *imply* connection: "Get through a whole winter without colds; take our pills." Ask a negative question to assume a positive answer: "Isn't quality the most important thing in an aspirin?"[19]

The techniques of subliminal manipulators have come to the attention of government officials. In 1974, Robert Pitofsky, Director of the Federal Trade Commission's Consumer Protection Bureau, listed four major concerns of the agency: "Advertising to children; television advertising that may unfairly exploit desires, fears, and anxieties; TV commercials where technical aspects of preparation may facilitate deception; and the consumer's physical, emotional, and psychological responses to advertising."[20] If government agencies and congressional reports are expressing grave concern over current advertising practices, shouldn't we?

Many of the messages that surround us would cause outrage if they were uncovered. We have personally witnessed subliminal messages of homosexuality, adultery, beastiality, death, Satan, skulls, bats, wolves, sexual organs, curse words, and many other offensive and insulting symbols. If you will take time to analyze the advertisements around you, the messages will eventually become crystal clear. This is the one thing the motivational manipulators fear, for if you recognize the technique, your conscious guard eliminates the subliminal impact on your behavior.

Chapter 5

RESULTS OF SUBLIMINAL SEDUCTION

Historian James Hitchcock states that the mass media is more responsible than anything else for the rise of secularism in our country.[1] Without the media's support, humanism could not possibly have made such an overwhelming inroad into an entire society in such a short period of time.

From 1965 to 1975, we experienced an extensive about-face in the basic underlying moral foundation of the country. One of the reasons behind this mass abandonment of traditional morality involves the system upon which advertising is based. The idea centers around our consumption of the merchandise all around us. Roughly, the idea states that the consumption of a product requires an adaptation of that product to our personal life. This adaptation changes us as we develop beliefs, attitudes, fears, hopes, and expectations that did not exist prior to the experience.

As we change, our society changes. The consumer—therefore, our society—gets it coming and going. Not only are we changed by the selling of a host of products but the very consumption of these products changes us and alters our perceptions. We are affected by the selling of the product, and we are affected by the consumption of the product. Is there any wonder why our society has undergone such a dramatic change in such a relatively short period of time?

Nothing is sacred or immune from the probing techniques of marketers who try to change our buying behavior. With the help of the social scientist, ad men probe our hidden weaknesses and then try to sell us everything from self-images to states of mind. They do not want us to make critical judgments of products; rather, we are expected to make subconscious emotional purchases. Our innermost being is the target. Over thirty years of advertising research has as its sole purpose the manipulation of consumer preferences. *All* marketing decisions are aimed to ultimately influence and change customer preferences. The implications of such manipulations are enormous. One researcher has called it the "first undertaking in mass behavior modification by coast-to-coast and intercontinental electronic hookup."[2]

When we take a closer look at how our attitudes are altered, we see that the constant saturation of media desensitizes us in certain areas (sex, violence, etc.). Different associations are given that eventually take the place of our previous attitudes. Things that once startled or offended us may now bring us humor. This type of conditioning has produced dangerous possibilities for our nation's future. One author questions, "What are the symbols that will call forth the citizen's allegiance, devotion, and reverential love?"[3] We should become even more alarmed when we realize that our children learn more about these types of values from TV than they do from school.

Another powerful tool of the mass media is its ability to define what is real and what isn't. This has become very important in today's world because there has been a significant breakdown in traditional institutions, such as the family, church, and school. Mass media is increasingly looked to for definitions of reality. Far too many people live according to a media image of happiness, and they try to imitate media stars.

We are told what to eat, what to wear, what is news, what is acceptable, what is good, what is bad—and many other values traditionally instilled by the family. Movies are known to exert a great influence in this respect. More and more, media is usurping the parental role in the education and socialization of children. And when it comes to training your kids, the media's motives are widely different than your own.

The list of media misinformation in human relationships is indeed a long one. Included in the danger are the magazine promises that imply all your problems will be solved in the marketplace. One psychoanalyst said marketers "often show fear of not being loved, and offer products to give you love."[4]

If we have come to look to products for our love and fulfillment, no wonder so many lonely and frustrated people inhabit the world. The nature of these messages is clear. Nicholas Johnson, while chairman of the Federal Communications Commission (FCC), said that advertising gives "people a phony set of values."[5]

To bring it even closer to home, your family is probably receiving its share of attacks. An average person sees 40,000 commercials a year. A pre-school child has spent more time in front of the TV set than a four-year college student has spent in the classroom.[6] All this time is spent soaking up values and lifestyles presented on the screen and is devoted to a medium that offers *us* as products to advertisers.

Marketers do not just want to *meet* demand, they want to *create* it and move up consumption through persuasion (often subliminally). One of the techniques used to do this involves creating images that nobody can attain naturally. For instance, a TV character is made to be macho, popular, good with women, etc. Of course the average person does not see this happening in his own daily life, so he sets out to become what he has been led to believe is natural and desirable. This is exactly what the manipulators want. They have already conveniently set up many ways for you to become your (really their) dream. All you have to do is buy the fancy car the hero drives, drink the same beer, buy the same hat, smoke the same brand, get the same haircut, or do a thousand other things that will take your money.

Ad men probe guilt, fear, anger, tension, loneliness, or anything else to create wants in consumers. Instead of soap, we buy beauty; instead of oranges, we buy vitality; and in place of our cars, we really buy prestige.[7] An advertising executive of a leading cosmetic firm stated that the company no longer followed women's desires, the company created them.[8] Images are deliberately set up at levels we cannot attain so we will have to buy the products offered to measure up and be accepted socially.

Don't think this isn't a powerful tool for modifying behavior. Many ads play on rejection, telling us we will be oddballs if we don't accept whatever image the ad is projecting. Nobody wants to be thought of as a fool, unaccepted by peers or society. Truly, the mass media industry is a vehicle used by the mass producers to *enforce* their reality upon us.

On the flip side, motivational research has led marketers to promise everything to the one who obeys their message (buy the product). Happiness, popularity, sex, fame, money, security, and any other need advertisers can pinpoint is promised to the unsuspecting consumer—if only he or she follows the pied pipers.

As you might guess, the list of products required to make oneself this "perfect" person goes on to infinity. And why not? This means you will be shelling out your hard-earned money for an endless supply of merchandise, all of which will be specifically created to fulfill your desires—*desires the advertisers gave you in the first place!*

For Sale: Your Innermost Secrets

Perhaps you are familiar with traditional marketing tools such as demographics. These are statistics that tell the advertiser valuable information about an area's population, age, income, etc. What you may not be familiar with is the new data that is being used more and more to formulate ad campaigns. It is called *psychographics.* This type of data strives to go beyond explaining who is buying; instead it is intended to explain *why* they are buying certain things. Housewives could be grouped into categories such as "outgoing, optimistic, apathetic, self-indulgent, contented cows, and worriers."9 No longer are you merely listed by age and income. Now your motivations, insecurities, and hidden weaknesses are listed to help manipulate your buying behavior.

For another example, men between the ages of twenty and forty could have been tested and found to have a high degree of insecurity regarding their male self-image. Suppose the researchers found that one third of all the men in this age bracket never played organized sports, are not physically active, and have not been successful in their relationships with women. These men could be targeted for any products subliminally laden with promises of "manhood." A typical result would be a car ad that shows a tough, good-looking young man picking up a gorgeous girl while onlookers stand by gazing with awe. The car is not being sold on the basis of its mechanical superiority but its appeal to the perceived inadequacy of the purchaser. This type of commercial is now in use.

The list would be too long to mention in its entirety, but some of the products marketed in this way include: cologne, liquor, electronic equipment, motorcycles, soft drinks, etc. In reality, these products have nothing to do with the hidden promises attached to them. Sex is only one thing being "sold" through advertising. Air conditioners, cake mixes, and motorboats are sold as promises of fulfillment, emotional security, reassurance of worth, ego gratification, love objects, sense of power, sense of roots, or immortality. Automobiles have distinct images and are often purchased as female surrogates, status reinforcements, virility, or ego fantasies. Think about the commercials you see every day. We are usually sold not a product but a feeling, an image, acceptance, sexual potency, popularity, and so on.[10]

Motivational researchers have discovered that feelings of insecurity lead to a desire for oral stimulation. Theories attempting to explain this reaction take us back to our infancy (breast feeding); but whatever the reason, this reaction is common in all of us. Think about what this type of information means to the marketer. Whenever feelings of insecurity are aroused, the first tendency is to put something in your mouth. How many commercials play on this fear of rejection? How many products offer us acceptance and popularity? Anything used orally qualifies: soft drinks, cigarettes, beer, food, candy, gum, etc. The ads for most of these products center on acceptance by a group of fun-loving, "beautiful people."

This type of manipulation has the potential to create tremendous frustration in the consumer. For example, could the overweight person really be motivated by a heart-felt desire to be accepted? Subconsciously, the person follows the "directions" of the marketers and eats. No wonder losing weight is so hard in our society. It is based on denying yourself the very thing that is fulfilling your need for acceptance—and this in order to *be* accepted!

Advertisers give products images and personalities. In one study on the image of cotton, women described the material as friendly, innocent, cool, calm, clean, and pure. The men in the survey had quite another impression. They called cotton cheap, without class, and without strength. Everything from cars to clothing is given a personality, and we purchase these things as "expressions of our innermost feelings."[11]

Another interesting aspect of merchandise is its *perceived morality* in the mind of the public. For instance, certain foods are considered morally bad while others are considered good. In one survey, milk was found to be thought of as the most perfect food. The "psychological meaning" of milk was found to be the beginning reason for this attitude. Researchers discovered that milk was "closely associated with emotional security." Reasons included the "infant-state milk experience, the effortlessness of drinking milk, and the parental and educational influences stressing the goodness of milk." Food has been deified by primative tribes and has become for us a medium of communication and a statement of social aspirations. Foods even have a perceived sex gender. Rice is considered feminine while potatoes are more masculine. Tea is feminine while coffee is masculine.[12] Armed with information like this, modern-day marketers have become experts in emotional manipulation and behavior modification.

As the true nature of advertising is uncovered, it becomes clear that many of the products we purchase are of no use to us. Some type of vulnerable need was pinpointed in us, and then a marketing strategy was developed to exploit that need. The subliminal and untrue promises of fulfillment can leave us in worse condition than before. But never fear, the manipulators surely have another empty promise just around the corner.

Subliminal messages have the power to change our value system. Each of us has reference points and standards by which we judge the world. Our reference points tell us whether a certain thing such as adultery is good or bad. Messages that bypass our conscious mind and hit the subconscious can actually move these points of reference.

If we find ourselves or our children becoming more and more accepting of so-called "alternative lifestyles," it is not just because we are becoming insensitive. Our value systems are slowly being manipulated by subliminal messages all around us that say things like, "adultery is acceptable." Lot never intended for his family to be lost over the corrupt values of Sodom and Gomorrah, but they were all deceived just the same. Unless we can know and recognize the hidden messages of evil influence, we cannot guard against them. God declared, "My people are destroyed for a lack of knowledge" (Hosea 4:6). The devil's number one tool is deception.

Advertising puts an associative link (of the product) in the minds of the consumer. These links "combine personal attitude toward life with the material things that embody them." Things can become our friends or our enemies. During World War II thousands of people faced prison rather than abandon their homes and possessions. Things become greater than simple inanimate objects. They become "expressions of our attitude toward life."[13] Because no belief or attitude comes from consciously perceived data, the subliminal links to merchandise put into our minds by advertisers actually become the basis for our life.

One of the founders of modern motivational research, Ernest Dichter, put it this way: "What we are witnessing is the development of a new value system. . . . We are rediscovering the old hedonism of the Greeks. . . . For better or worse, this type of social and economic climate erodes our traditional puritanical thinking. What is happening is that the concept of original sin is being undermined, proved to be false. . . . Not only is self-denial not in style any longer, it has already become something to be ridiculed."[14] These words were very perceptive, especially to have been written in the early 60's. Now in the 1980's, we can see that this is exactly what has happened to our nation.

As a last note before proceeding to other areas, you should know that the person most influenced by these subliminal techniques could be you! There seems to be a correlation between how much the message would offend you and how much it affects you. In other words, vulgarity painted in the shadows of a picture would tend to have *more* of a subliminal influence on people who believe it is evil. Therefore, Christians and moral people in general would make the most inviting targets for the "fiery darts" of subliminal manipulation.

PICTORAL SECTION

Subliminal Figures And Words In Ads

Figure 1. The word "sex" is painted into the ice cubes of this Gilbey's Gin advertisement.

Figure 2. This apparently innocent get-together takes on new meanings under close examination. The broken putter is positioned to extend from the standing man's genital area. All others are looking, reaching, and reacting to it with their mouths open. In the background two men are shown. One is looking downward, and the other is obviously standing at the urinal. In this ad, with its homosexual overtones, all attention is directed toward the genital area. In the shadow of the bottle a figure that appears to be a nude female can be seen.

Figure 3. One would expect a surprised look on the bather's face if someone had jumped into the water splashing him. Why would he have a look of terror? The barracuda-like creature painted into the splash is giving him plenty of reason to be terrified. Notice where it is going to bite him. Other figures in the splash include a man, penis, older man, and a remarkable likeness to the *Star Wars* character, Darth Vader.

Phallic Symbols In Advertising

Figure 4. While this illustration may be offensive to some, it is included to prove the depth of morally perverse material some marketers will use. This type of message is not just back-masked on rock music albums. You are also a target of subliminal manipulation.

This ad features an independent and self-assured woman. Just above her beltline a male organ has been subliminally painted. The advertisement is working on the recently created insecurity in women that stems from the tremendous pressure our society has demanded. Today's woman must be the perfect mother and wife, as well as have a successful career in the male-dominated business world. For the woman who feels guilty about a lack of success in these areas, this product offers both "manhood" and success.

If traditionally male attributes are demanded of all females, there will inevitably be insecurity created somewhere along the line. Since we know insecurity leads to oral stimulation, a cigarette is the natural choice to "fulfill" this deep-seated need. The drive to buy this product may be motivated by a desire for independence, security, toughness, success, and manhood—all stirred up by marketers who know our weaknesses and how to exploit them.

Religious Symbols In Ads

Figure 5. The children have their hands raised in worship or praise to, of all things, television monitors!

Figure 6. We should only let one Spirit move us, and it certainly isn't the spirit the marketing manipulators are offering.

Figure 7. This unfortunate man doesn't need cologne; he needs deliverance.

Sexual Overtones

Figures 8 & 9. These ads speak for themselves.

Figure 10. What looks like a vibrator, works like a vibrator, and is designed for "your most delicate area"?

Figure 11 & 12. Public exhibitionism is the theme of this national ad campaign.

Figure 13. As the public's attitude toward sex

loses the inhibitions of traditional morality, more and more deviant suggestions must be used to bring the same reaction.

Popular Music

Figure 14. Ozzy Osbourne, formerly of Black Sabbath; Boy George, drag queen; Twisted Sister—MTV video promotes physical abuse of parents; Prince—songs include topics such as incest.

Figure 15. Pentagrams, satanic images, evil messages, and perverted lifestyles are common in today's popular music.

Figure 16. This decal is typical of the many posters and paraphernalia available over-the-counter to children of all ages.

Figure 17. We found this product advertised in a nationwide drug store chain. Notice the titles of the "Psychic Series."

Figure 1

Figure 2

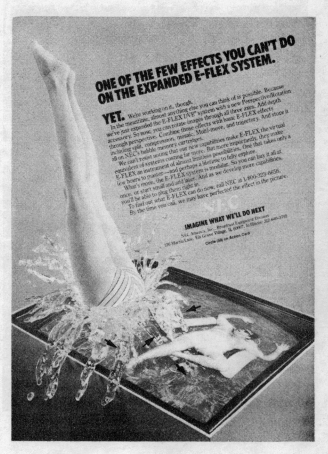

Figure 3

Figure 4

Figure 5

Figure 6

Introducing Quorum. A cologne for the other man lurking inside you.

Eau de toilette,
spray cologne,
after shave.

Figure 7

Figure 8

SEAGRAM'S GIN.

"They say it's the number one gin in America.

They say you can taste the difference.

They say it's exceptional with tonic."

"They also say it's improving your vocabulary ...in body language."

Everything they say...is true.
SEAGRAM'S. AMERICA'S NUMBER ONE GIN.

Figure 9

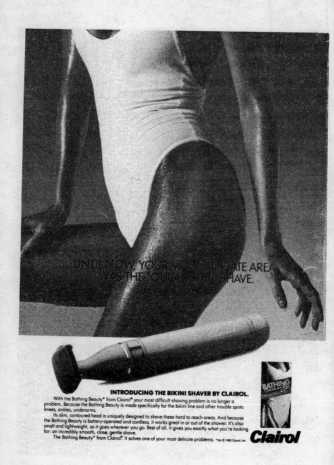

UNTIL NOW, YOUR MOST DELICATE AREA
WAS THE TOUGHEST TO SHAVE.

INTRODUCING THE BIKINI SHAVER BY CLAIROL.

With the Bathing Beauty* from Clairol* your most difficult shaving problem is no longer a
problem. Because the Bathing Beauty is made specifically for the bikini line and other trouble spots:
knees, ankles, underarms.

Its slim, contoured head is uniquely designed to shave these hard to reach areas. And because
the Bathing Beauty is battery-operated and cordless, it works great in or out of the shower. It's also
small and lightweight, so it goes wherever you go. Best of all, it gives you exactly what you're looking
for: an incredibly smooth, close, gentle shave.

The Bathing Beauty* from Clairol.* It solves one of your most delicate problems. *TM © 1985 Clairol, Inc.

Clairol

Figure 10

Figure 11

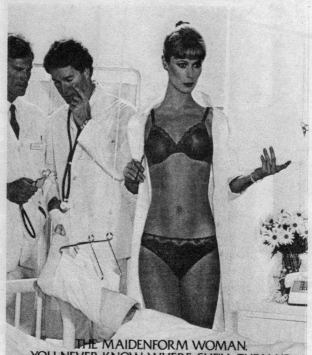

Figure 12

Meet the Diors: the Wizard, the Mouth, and Oliver. When they were good they were very, very good and when they were bad they were gorgeous.

Figure 13

Figure 14a

Figure 14b

Figure 14c

Figure 14d

Figure 15a

Figure 15b

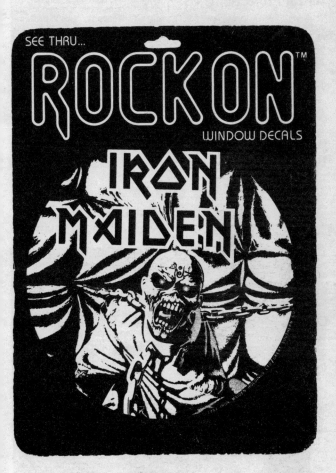

Figure 16

_____Psychic

Astral Projection

In consciousness classes I have conducted, numerous people were able to successfully complete their first astral trip. Prior to taking the class, many of these people had absolutely no awareness of the concept at all. In this tape, I have taken the programming that has proven successful, and added an extra dimension of sound to make it more effective. Allow two weeks to prepare—using this tape—and you, too, can join the increasing number of people who are experiencing out-of-body experiences.

Birth Separation

The birth experience for most people is so traumatic that it represents the closest we have ever been to death. Birth trauma could be the source of asthma, headaches, depression and body aches. Try this test: inhale deeply and hold it. If you find yourself pulling in your stomach when you inhale, your body mechanism is backwards, probably due to birth trauma. If you desire, this tape could help correct your breathing and release the negative feelings that surround your birth.

Chakra Meditation

By balancing and harmonizing the energies of your chakras, you unleash incredible cosmic and psychic powers, powers that benefit all mankind. This tape can help.

Conception

This tape is designed for those couples who wish to have a child, but are experiencing difficulty in consummating the pregnancy. This tape can also assist those couples who wish to go beyond conception and attract a high soul.

Develop Your Psychic Abilities

Each of us possesses some degree of ESP. True, some have developed it to a higher degree than others. Yet, I know from personal experience that you can develop far beyond your present capability. In doing so, you will enrich your life greatly. To me, ESP is the power that makes life run smoothly.

Parallel Lives— Separate Selves

THE EDUCATION OF OVERSOUL 7, by Jane Roberts, introduces the exciting concept that a soul may be expressing more than one life at a time. You can test this concept for yourself. Are you experiencing life in more than one time and place at this very moment? Why not? The only limitations that exist are the ones you accept. Your potential is unlimited.

Past Life Regression with Mate or Lover

Have you lived a former life with your present mate or lover? Sometimes, you may get that feeling—and rightly so. We tend to return to life surrounded by those persons who will afford us the greatest opportunity for spiritual growth. We often change sexes, nationalities, religions, and family position. The past often holds the key to understanding the present. Explore your past life relationship(s) with your mate or lover and add meaning and understanding to your present life experience.

Past Life Regression

Fascinated by your past? Have you lived before? If so, where? What time? Who were you? Man or woman? I have successfully guided many people into their past lives to gain a better understanding of their present life. The techniques used on this tape can be very effective.

Past Life Therapy

"An eye for an eye, a tooth for a tooth!" "What ye sow, so shall ye

Figure 17a

Series

reap." The law of cause and effect: Karma. The experiences that we plant in our past lives are harvested within four lives of that experience. Some harvest adversity, pain, hardship and physical or mental problems. It is possible to reconstruct your present life by releasing yourself of all the negativity of the past. The Law of Grace can be invoked to release you from the Law of Karma.

Psychic Healing

We could be capable of healing our own body and the bodies of others. Your thoughts, actions, and beliefs have a profound effect upon those around you who suffer from illness. This tape can make you a positive influence. I will guide you, step-by-step, through the mental process necessary for psychic repair. Follow it, and I guarantee satisfaction.

Psychic Protection

On this tape, I give you those techniques and methods that are necessary to safeguard the integrity of your mind. When you open up pyschically, you also open the doors to certain negative forces and influences. you must be able to protect yourself against these unwanted intruders.

Talents/Abilities from Past Life

Generally, it takes more than one lifetime to become a master in any single area of accomplishment. Whether it be a boxer, writer, doctor, parent or hypnotist, one life builds upon another. Use this tape to bring to your conscious awareness the knowledge of your past talents and abilities. These abilities can enable you to discover your life's real purpose.

Time Traveller

For years, I have guided people through the pages of history into time and space, to expand their awareness of the world in which they live. Now, you can experience Atlantis, and open the secret passageway in the Sphinx and journey into the treasure room. There is also a mysterious adventure awaiting you on a spaceship. Use this tape. Please let me know where your journeys take you.

Visualization—Aura Reading

Some come by it naturally, while others must practice to develop the skill of visualization. One of the keys to creating your own reality is mastering the art of visualization. An additional benefit can be your ability to see and read auras.

Where is My Parent?
(The Adopted Child)

Where is My Child?
(The Natural Parent)

How many times have you anticipated a phone call, a letter, or meeting someone? This same experience that seems to happen by chance can be applied to help you find your parent/child. If you would like to search out your parent/child, these tapes are designed to help you in your search.

World Peace

Mother Earth is wounded. She has put up with our barbaric behavior, insensitivity and general lack of awareness much too long. Individually and/or collectively, WE are responsible for the conditions of our planet. Our thinking affects the weather, tides, temperature and the earth's shifts. One person—YOU—can make a difference. Bring two or three people together and form a triangle of energy. Use this tape as your guide. Return the planet to a Garden of Eden where love, light, and life abound!

Figure 17b

Chapter 6

CONFLICT OF INTERESTS

The mass media has become America's entertainer, informer, and advocate. Rarely does the mass media report on the conflict of interests dwelling within its own ranks. The basic purpose of mass media and advertising is *not* to inform the public or to protect the "little guy" from exploitation by big business and government. The basic goal of mass media is to make money. *Profit* is what the media is all about.

Advertising and media have become essential ingredients in our economic system. They are controlled by extremely powerful corporations that have shareholders like any other profit-making enterprise. All three television networks own other businesses. CBS owns Creative Playthings; X-acto Tools; Steinway Pianos; Holt, Rinehart, and Winston book publishers; and a number of magazines.[1] Most of the news and entertainment we receive is produced by a few major corporations. Newscasters, directors, and writers are *employees* of big business—just like the typical corporate executive they pretend to "protect" us from.

To give you an idea of the money involved, a thirty-second television commercial in prime time can currently bring in over $100,000. That is not counting the cost to produce the spot. In the early 70's, a full-page magazine ad would cost over $50,000. By 1978, the three television networks made over $4 billion in advertising revenue.[2]

A recent edition of *Newsweek* reported a probable purchase of ABC.[3] The price tag: $3.5 billion. The buyers were attracted by the growth prospects and *large cash flow*. The magazine article estimated the selling price of CBS around $4.2 billion, and RCA would bring in an incredible $5 billion. The advertising industry in the United States alone brought in over $87 billion in 1984.[4] Don't be fooled by misleading images. Enormous sums of money are involved, and the mass media is indeed big business.

Now that we have established the bottom line in media, the conflict of interests inherent in the system should be clear.

Take, for example, the popular show, *60 Minutes*. Each week the "crusaders" of the news world lead us down the path of "social justice." We are supposed to believe these journalists are actually uncovering the "bad guys" of the business world and championing the cause of the common man. Baloney! This program is really show-biz making big bucks by delivering a large audience to high-financed advertisers.

When was the last time you saw an expose on the average salaries of TV news correspondents? For Washington, it is $90,000.[5] Some news correspondents are making $300,000 and more. You may have heard of the $1 million annual salary Barbara Walters is making, but did you know that Dan Rather made $1.6 million back in 1980?[6] The next time you watch the CBS nightly news, remember that the man talking is a multi-millionaire employed by a huge corporation worth billions. Is there a conflict of interests in the mass media? The next time you want to know the truth about deceptive advertising, try asking *60 Minutes*.

Chapter 7

POWER IN THE WRONG HANDS

Control of the mass media brings with it enormous power. The average American home has the television set on fifty hours each week—more than a normal work-week.[1] With a show like *60 Minutes* bringing in thirty-six million viewers, and with most Americans trusting television as their most believable news source, the potential for abuse rises ominously.

Not only the most trusted source, TV is also the most looked-to source for news. Thirty-four million people watch it daily.[2] The situation has deteriorated to the point that "without the news media, we know almost nothing outside our own sphere of activity."[3] For better or worse, television has become our window to the world.

The vast majority of our news and entertainment comes from only five corporations: ABC, CBS, NBC, UPI, and AP. Broadcast material from these companies turns the U.S. into a "vast neighborhood" and thereby changes our society. TV has become a cultural revolution. If we live in the mountains, it is there. If we go to the ocean, it is there—shaping, molding, and changing our entire nation. And although there is an incredible power to manipulate our society, no regulations or licenses govern the production activity of these huge corporations. Still, the American public continues to trust the media for accuracy.

Rose Goldsen, in her excellent book, *The Show And Tell Machine,* states, "Access to television gives those who have it and those who buy it unprecedented power and privilege to show and tell all of us over and over again their own views of propriety and impropriety, to express their own attitudes and modes of speech, beaming out lessons in their own customs, their own values, their own life-styles, their own slants on reality. The rest of us have no equivalent opportunity to show and tell ours."[4] Many experts feel that the medium shapes the outcome of everything from elections at home to crisis abroad, and we have granted it the "power to redefine our place and our social reality."[5]

The media elite, those controlling what goes out over the media, are generally liberal or left liberal. They believe that conservatives are irrational or psychologically malfunctioning. They also believe that the answers for our society are found in good will and intellect—all institutions not based on rationality should be eliminated. With this comes a strong distrust for the military and the police. Are these the people you want controlling your "window" to the world?

The media elite are "extraordinarily powerful, able to defy and persuade a political elite which they can destroy."[6] In 1978, Aleksandr Solzhenitsyn observed, "The press has become the greatest power within Western countries, more powerful than the legislative, the executive, the judiciary."[7] A recent example of this occurred when Dan Rather "negotiated" with Lebanese minister Nabih Berri concerning the hostages in Beirut. This happened in spite of the fact that other sources had clearly shown Berri's involvement in the actual abduction of the hostages. Did you vote for Dan Rather to represent us?

When this opportunity to reach masses of people is combined with subliminal technology, the prospects are Orwellian. Truly, the motivational analyst and the symbol manipulator make a disturbing team. When subliminal techniques are employed in politics and public opinion, the potential is very dangerous. "The goal is mind molding itself. No longer is the aim just to play on our subconscious to persuade us to buy a refrigerator or a new motorboat that we may not need. The aim now is nothing less than to influence the state of our mind and to channel our behavior as citizens."[8] This clearly invades our privacy and interferes with our freedom of choice. How far will the media elite go in molding our reality and changing our behavior? Read on.

Currently, a very dangerous marketing research activity combines the mass media, business establishments, computers, and the use of personal identification cards.[9] This system, in over 30,000 homes, brings a fresh meaning to Revelation 13:16-17. People fill out personal information forms, which, in turn, are entered into a master computer. The computer issues a card to the consumer, complete with the invisible marked magnetic strip. A computer also monitors the television activity of the home via the local cable company's split-run technology.

Every time a person buys from participating local businesses, the purchase is recorded in the computer. By combining the monitoring of viewing habits with the monitoring of buying habits, the marketers have the perfect system for testing new advertising campaigns. Different commercials are inserted into different viewing areas of the community by the cable company, and the effect is computed according to buying changes. They know what we watch and what we buy!

The potential dangers of such a system are acknowledged even by secular sources. One representative of a civil liberties union raised a disturbing question: What if a community under such a system had only one grocery store?[10] Citizens could be *required* to use the ID card for purchases. This bears repeating. A card with an identifying mark is used to purchase products. This enables all buying decisions to be monitored. All television activity is also monitored by a split-run system of the local cable company. People have *willingly* submitted to such a system today. Will the day soon arrive when the choice is in another's hands?

The Wrong Hands?

Tremendous power lies in mass media. Is it in the wrong hands? We have already discussed the attitudes and values of the media elite. They are politically liberal, pro-abortion, pro-homosexual, and natural enemies of conservative religious groups.[11]

Perhaps we have no better illustration of this than the words of one of the founders of consumer motivational research, Ernest Dichter. In his book, *Handbook Of Consumer Motivations,* Dichter stated his belief that the more products we consume, the richer our life becomes. He declares that morality is relative and should be approached in "a scientific fashion rather than a theological one." This man, who has been very influential in modern advertising strategy, readily admits to manipulating consumer attitudes and morality. We "often have, when dealing with activities that arouse guilt feelings, the problem of offering *absolution* and giving the subject the *permission* to indulge."[12]

What an incredible privilege to be able to enter the subconscious of the American people and offer absolution for immoral behavior! Is this power in the wrong hands? You decide.

Chapter 8

YOUR CHILDREN: TARGETS

Television has assumed a major role in raising our children. It saturates their minds during the formative years and has brought about such a change in our society that some feel we may be past the point of no return. "The imagers have already dominated the thought-environment of the country's first television generation. No society based on reason and democratic forms of control is likely to survive equivalent domination a second time around."[1] These are strong words coming from researchers in this area. What makes them come to such a conclusion?

On the average, a child between the ages of three and twelve spends more than 1,000 hours per year watching TV. As we have stated, the "average preschool age child is estimated to have absorbed more hours of unstructured TV input than the hours an average student at a liberal arts college spends for four full years in the classroom."[2] During one year, a child will see a total of 22,000 ads and will be subjected to over 200 hours of commercials.[3]

This educational "opportunity" concerning our children has not gone unnoticed. For TV alone, more than $800 million a year is spent on ads directed toward children. Children are urged to "wheedle, whine, or harangue their way to new acquisitions."[4] This is not without good reason. At least $30 million weekly, or $1.5 billion yearly, is added onto grocery bills just to accomodate childrens' desires.

Children play a major role in choosing family food. One survey concluded that children determine how 37 percent of the family food budget is spent. Of course, this causes constant friction in the family. As "long as children are both financially dependent on their parents and exposed to a spectacle of consumer temptations, the disfunction between their 'needs' and their families' incomes will regularly generate child outlaws. . . . Nothing undermines parental affection more decisively than a trip to the supermarket with a couple of TV-wise junior consumers."[5]

Teenage population declined between 1975 and 1980, but their spending rose more than 50 percent! Even with this decline, children under the age of thirteen make up more than one-fourth of our population, numbering more than 50 million. Almost all of these children are receiving more time in front of the TV than they are in school. With this massive TV time comes commercials, most of them directed specifically to children.[6]

Many authorities are becoming concerned over this socialization of our nation's youth. "Some psychologists have long been convinced that the conduct of actors appearing in television shows—for better or worse—become models of behavior for children. Parents, too, have expressed concern that violence on television may not only throw their children's behavior off-center but may have an adverse effect on their emotional growth and development."[7]

Another author concludes that ads "do furnish a vision of a type of lifestyle which many people will desire to emulate or identify with."[8] This is even more dangerous when it is realized that most advertising (wherever directed) is based on adult perception. Kids receive impressions of reality from advertising that exceed their skill in understanding them logically.

If you feel that the upbringing of your children is slipping from your control, you are correct. One advertising "authority" suggested these ways to handle the youth market: "Treat youth with authority; 'protect' them; 'control' them; tell them what to do. Basically they're insecure . . . reassure them in advertising copy."[9] Sounds very much like parental responsibility, doesn't it?

Other studies confirm that TV eliminates much of the opportunity for interaction between parents and their children: "The television set casts its magic spell, freezing speech and action, turning the living into silent statues so long as the enchantment lasts. The primary danger of the television screen lies . . . in the behavior it prevents . . . the family festivities and arguments through which much of the child's learning takes place and through which his character is formed. Turning on the television set can turn off the process that transforms children into people."[10]

Just what is this "surrogate parent" teaching our children? As far as nutrition and health, children are being "programmed to demand sugar and sweetness in every food . . . and are being counter-educated away from nutrition knowledge. A child watching 73 spots in a total of 200 minutes of Saturday television would gather (1) that cereals with sugar are great energy sources; (2) that energy and action are equivalent to happiness; and (3) that ability and health are a product of eating ready-to-eat, preferably sweet, cereals."[11]

In regard to family relationships, kids are fed an alarming distortion. The majority of cartoons portray no family ties. The gang is usually the source for stability. Soap operas also have become a major source for socialization. Many housewives expose their young children to the images and sounds of the soaps all day long. These kids can not only tell you what the soaps are all about, but they identify with the characters. Can you imagine a generation coming to power that patterns life after the world of the soaps?

One out of two parents surveyed felt that their children learned most about sexuality from television. The sexual values and attitudes seen on television seem very real to young children.

What is TV teaching our children about sex? Sex on TV is generally portrayed as a game, seldom as a beautiful and meaningful relationship between husband and wife. "Most references to intercourse on television, whether verbally insinuated or contextually implied, occur between unmarried partners (5 times as often as married couples); references to intercourse with prostitutes comes in second." Today, children will learn about topics such as adultery, pre-marital sex, abortion, and homosexuality from the media.[12]

Role models are also important in a young person's development. Women on TV are shown to get their way by being seductive, slinky, or wearing revealing clothes. The role of housewife is shown to be boring and a real chore. Men seldom show a need for affection or a warm relationship. The elderly are frequently treated with disrespect and are shown as useless, stubborn, foolish, and asexual.[13] In comic books, seven out of ten characters commit some crime. Killers represent thirteen percent of the population. In more than one half of the stories, the key to superstatus is the consumption of a chemical substance.[14]

USA Today described in their November 1983 publication a "frightening impact of television on school children." In November 1977, *The Saturday Evening Post* reported that kids lose the ability to learn from reality because life-experiences are much more complicated than the ones they see on the screen. Many reports confirm that television violence is linked to aggressive behavior in children.[15] "Many parents also cite with horror the statistics that during the estimated 22,000 hours in front of television by the age of fourteen, a child has witnessed the assault on or destruction of 18,000 individuals."[16]

Media violence and destructive behavior have been linked in several cases, such as the fourteen-year-old who hung himself after becoming an avid viewer of rock star Alice Cooper's mock suicide. After seeing the movie, *Dirty Harry,* the night before, a young boy from Ohio shot his brother while playing a *game* of "Dirty Harry." An eleven-year-old from Illinois strangled a four-year-old girl after getting the idea from television.[17]

We usually think of TV as a pacifier or babysitter, but it is also an educator and value giver. "Television . . . saturates the thought environment with images and stories it selects. . . . They install themselves in . . . imaginations. There they reside as models forming the categories of thought that make thinking possible. It is minds they make."[18] Another researcher flatly states, "There exists no single or multiple mechanism available to modern man which holds such a devastating potential for brain-washing, mass programming, and the destruction of individualism."[19]

Yes, your children are targets. Campaigns financed with millions of dollars seek to change your child's behavior. Perhaps most alarming, with this power, mass media leaders have continually asserted a prerogative to operate free and independent of other institutions, such as the church or the family. Guard your loved ones, for your adversary goes about as a roaring lion, seeking whom he may devour. (See 1 Peter 5:8.)

Chapter 9

UNREALITY

Children are not the only targets of mass media manipulation. Think for a moment of the impact mass media has on the world around us. Our clothes are largely the result of the fashion of the day, usually promoted by magazines and TV. Hardly anything escapes the influence of mass media. Our speech is affected. Our transportation, household furnishings, comedy, hairstyles, music, leisure activity, peer groups, and even our choices in pets are heavily influenced by advertisers and mass media.

Our very *reality* is largely determined by what we see and hear. Consumers actively use advertising and merchandise as the material for their own "reality." If the communication of advertisers and the products they offer become the building blocks for our reality, then our reality is in serious trouble.

Some state that the task ahead for advertisers is the reconciliation of appearance and reality. The trouble is, advertisers don't want to reconcile their images (appearance) to reality. *They want to change our reality to fit their images!* As we have seen in previous chapters, marketers have long since departed from merely following the conditions that exist. They don't just *meet* demand, they *create* it and thereby alter our attitudes and preferences.

When people change, society changes. "The TV machine regulates time, channelizes or unifies perceptual experience, and establishes (all subliminally) an entire range of desirable expectations, value systems, identities, relationships, and perspectives toward the entire world. The tube has already become the primary source of information for a majority of the North American, if not the world's, population."[1]

Rose Goldsen adds that "many aspects of mass behavior are quite easily manipulable through the power of suggestion. They should remind us further that at best only a blurry and highly permeable line separates what we think of as an objectively real world from a metaphoric one that arresting arrangements of images and sound can plunge us into."[2]

Television actually becomes another member of the family and brings its "own view of the world, its own interpretations of reality, its own images and symbolic forms." This force can become so strong that the imaginary relationships we have with celebrities on the screen can equal our real relationships. "Many people have difficulty distinguishing between fantasy relationships and reality, and that can go haywire, as in the case of John Hinckley and his imaginary relationship with actress Jodie Foster."

Celebrities have become our role models and the "gods of our culture." This indulgence is expected to grow worse as media increases in power. People are demanding greater and greater experiences in the fantasy that media provides.[3]

The more we watch television, the harder it is to distinguish between reality and imagery. "Exposure to television for hours every day simply further separates youngsters from the world of reality."[4] One report suggested that our society needs stability and commonality, which the mass media provides. This may be true, but unfortunately for us, the window of the world as seen in the media is limited and tainted. TV events are *unreality*, only pieces of a spectacle, "imitations, visual impressions of something reflected; optical images converted to electronic images that are still empty reflections of a real world which we know little."[5]

A camera catches only superficialities, or fleeting impressions. A photograph is filled with misconceptions. In a September 1982 article entitled, "The Seductive Picture Show," Joe Saltzman of *USA Today* goes on to add that what "is bothersome is our continuing belief that what that camera catches is reality, is truth, is the way things really are. It soothes us. It replaces reality."

What does all this mean to our families? As the role of media in our children's development increases, less participation is available for the parent. Values in programs seem remarkably real and provide social and emotional identification for children.

A National Institute of Mental Health publication reported that "the single most important aspect of a child's sexual learning is the set of messages children—indeed all of us—receive throughout life about 'appropriate' masculine and feminine attributes and roles."[6] The report goes on to state that media does indeed affect sexual socialization. In other words, the "reality" of the media is gradually becoming the reality for our children and for us all.

Even news/information programs change reality. Material is invented, facts are bent, and crucial information is often omitted. One television producer revealed that "news is a variety show scheduled and paced like a vaudeville show."[7] For sitcoms, the audience is prompted by the use of signs, and audience reaction is usually sweetened in post-production. What you see is rarely what actually took place.

In all of this misrepresentation, remember that "experiments have established most emphatically that as a training device, or if you will, a brainwashing or conditioning device, television has enormous potential."[8] With this in mind, let's take a closer look at the message that "conditions" us.

We are being taught that it is normal to solve problems through violence, that happiness is found through consumption, and that being a consumer is attractive.[9] Sexual desirability is determined by our relationship to consumer goods with their associated fantasies. Television values include narcis-

75

sism: the immediate gratification of wants, the power to control others, and the humanistic teaching of the goodness of man. Our self-respect has been changed to pride.[10]

We see more violence, and we are less moved by it. TV crime is *ten times* greater than in real life. Pain, suffering, or medical help rarely follows violence on the screen. A major theme for soap operas is sickness and turmoil, although hardly anyone dies a natural death. Incredibly, soaps have become one of the most sought after sources for medical advice![11]

It is dangerous to " . . . construct our experience and substitute media world for real world so that we are becoming less and less able to make the fine value judgments that a complex world requires."[12] Commercial TV "is changing us more toward accepting as reality a mindless, spiritless, distorted perception of life than it is toward deepening our understanding of what is truly real."[13] We see, but we do not understand, we never have time to listen, to think, to ask questions, to get answers."[14]

Unfortunately, the bottom line for today's media child is, "Just don't think about it."

Chapter 10

PLANNED OBSOLESCENCE

An interesting note in the advertising area involves the idea of "planned obsolescence." In Vance Packard's book, *The Hidden Persuaders,* he says that in the early 50's marketers were faced with an ugly fact. Consumers already had many of the household appliances that marketers wanted to unload. The answer? *Psychological obsolescence.*[1] The strategy was simple: make the public style-conscious, then frequently update styles. When you think about it, you will realize that we've gone along with it ever since!

A General Motors employee later came up with the term "dynamic obsolescence." In the automobile industry, dynamic obsolescence means that "the exterior of the car will be frequently changed so that the car appears old a year after it was made, that the insides will be so flimsy that the car will indeed grow old before its time, and that each year a pretense of dramatic improvement will be made. The cost of dynamic obsolescence is passed on to the buyer twice: first, by tacking the cost of style changes on to the price of the car (about 25% of the price), and second, in the car's unnecessarily rapid loss of value."[2]

Along with the manipulation of the consumer, materials have been cheapened in the competition of the marketplace. "Here the con game is played with abandon. Products are meant to wear out so they will have to be replaced. Parts are priced so as to make them more economical to replace than to repair."[3] "The automobile hustle by now has assumed gigantic proportions. It is a fair estimate that the American as car owner is swindled each year out of more money than the average man earns in the poorest parts of the world." One estimate concludes that the average car owner works more than four and a half hours a day or more than 1,500 hours a year to provide for his transportation.[4]

Consumer Reports magazine reported an average of thirty-six defects per car on the 1973 models they tested. This shoddy construction passes benefits all the way down the line. "The repair shop will get more business; the manufacturer will sell more monopoly-priced parts; lawyers will do more lawyering; and the insurance men will write higher premiums."[5]

We should also add that advertisers will get more accounts if there is a high turnover, regardless of the reason. The purpose here is not to pick on the automobile industry. A number of industries could have been chosen. *Made in the U.S.A.* was synonomous with quality in days gone by. Now foreign manufacturers lead the way in attention to detail. Let's not blame the American worker—let's look to the creator of "dynamic obsolescence."

Years ago, the manipulation of the American consumer began. He was encouraged to forget old inhibitions, splurge, and charge things on credit. The "me" generation was born. Fashions changed more frequently, music became a whirlwind of activity, technology increased, and "fast" food was born. The phrase, "If it feels good, do it," described perfectly the philosophy of a new generation of Americans. Even our relationships have become throw-away: more than half of the marriages in our country now end in divorce.

The intrusion into the subconscious of the American public might have had its monetary rewards, but the long-term results are devastating. It is time to teach our children the truth. We, the consumer, have, to a large extent, been played for fools.

Chapter 11

THE BEAT GOES ON

"Atmospheres are going to come through music because music is a spiritual thing of its own. You can hypnotize people with music, and when you get people to their weakest point you can preach into the subconscious what you want to say." These are the words of the late rock and roll legend, Jimmie Hendrix.[1]

Music is a powerful force in today's youth culture. The average teen listens to more than six hours of rock music a day. Whatever rock music is saying, it is obviously reaching the hearts and minds of our nation's young people. Many messages are being absorbed through this medium. Dr. John Diamond states that "no parental or police restraint is likely to override a suggestion made through effective hypnosis if it is implanted firmly and often enough on a subject in a receptive sensitized state."[2] If Jimmie Hendrix and Dr. Diamond are correct, whatever rock music is implanting into the minds of receptive fans is more powerful than parental or legal restraint.

The message of much of today's music is shocking. Sex and drugs are two recurrent themes throughout a great deal of contemporary music. Everything from Eric Clapton's song, "Cocaine," to Madonna's recent hit, "Like A Virgin," reinforces a constant barrage of the old slogan, "sex, drugs, and rock n' roll."

We take it for granted that you know about this message in popular music. If you question this in any way, please take a few minutes to visit a record shop and look through the albums. You will immediately notice the blatant anti-social messages throughout the musical merchandise. Another message should begin to disturb your consciousness— a message of great danger to our society and, in particular, a great danger to your children.

The message of eminent danger we specifically want to expose involves the supernatural. Musical messages today are extremely religious in many instances. The rock group Black Sabbath has been known to hold black masses before their concerts, including sprinkling a nude with animal blood on an altar. Ritchie Blackmore, formerly of Deep Purple, admits to regularly holding seances to get closer to "god" and astrally projecting out of his body during concerts to mingle spiritually with the crowd. One album of the Rolling Stones was called *Their Satanic Majesties Request,* on which the group posed as witches. Their song, "Sympathy For The

Devil," has become the unofficial national anthem for satanists.[3]

Occult messages are becoming more and more prevalent in the popular music of today. Jimmie Hendrix was heavily involved in the demonic supernatural and claimed to come from an asteroid belt. Jimmy Page of Led Zeppelin runs his own occult bookstore and now lives in the mansion of the late British spiritualist, Alister Crowley.[4] The group Blue Oyster Cult is very upfront with their satanic messages. In their hit, "Don't Fear The Reaper," kids are encouraged to embrace Satan, who they say is "our father who art in heaven." KISS is noted for firebreathing, sadomasochism, and vomiting blood on stage.

We could talk about Meatloaf's album, *Bat Out Of Hell*, or Alice Cooper, who claims to be the reincarnation of a 17th century witch, or AC/DC's song "Highway To Hell"—but you are getting the message. The theme, sex, drugs, and rock and roll, is now being extended to include Satan. The ever-increasing message of rock music today is that the supernatural is available to all kids and that the door into the supernatural is the occult.

The lead singer for Meatloaf admits that when he gets on stage he is possessed. Jim Steinman says, "It's almost like Hitler . . . because . . . they're mesmerized by the music. They have the audience hypnotized. They could say, 'We're going out there and lift up this building,' and they'd just lift it up. That's the kind of control they have."[5]

When the entire picture is understood, it can be a frightening situation. Music is the perfect medium for subliminal messages, and the messages that are being promoted include an invitation into the supernatural realm of satanic manifestations.

As well as being a perfect medium for subliminal messages, music is also an avenue for social awareness and cultural change. This is evident in the lifestyle and clothes that are in fashion today. Many of the styles originate in the music industry. Music forms consciousness and binds people together. David Crosby of Crosby, Stills, Nash, and Young, said, "I figured the only thing to do was to swipe their kids. By saying that, I'm not talking about kidnapping, I'm talking about changing their value system which removes them from their parents' world very effectually."[6]

With statements such as these, why do we need to look for backward masking? Books have been written specifically about this technique, and they are important works; but there are enough blatant, upfront messages to let us know the true nature of much of today's music. The main point is not whether the words are forward or backward, the point is that the music opens the door to the subconscious, letting *any* message (however bad) come in. Unfortunately, as we have seen, the message is overwhelmingly evil—for our children and our country.

Chapter 12

LAUGHING AT YOU

Comedy has become a big part of our culture. Nine out of the top ten television shows are situation comedies.[1] Eight out of ten viewers tuned in to watch the last episode of *MASH*, one of the most popular programs of all time. *Saturday Night Live, SCTV, Late Night With David Letterman, Monty Python,* and many others have become a major factor in today's youth culture, providing most of the material for peer group humor and conversation.

Ridicule and the absurd have become popular conversational styles. Anyone who has worked around youth knows about this new humor. Unless your child is unusually independent, this new brand of humor is influencing him or her through peer group pressure. One author goes so far as to say, "A social policy has evolved for the shaping of the public's sense of humor."[2]

Before we look closer at the nature of today's comedy, it is interesting to note common characteristics in the comedians themselves. An article in

Psychology Today describes comedians as "brilliant, angry, paranoiac, fearful, and depressed. They don't know if they're devils or angels, and they engage in comedy to avoid destroying themselves."[3] Is this really the type of character you want making "social policy" for your children?

Humor in itself has always been subject to certain criticism. Many analysts say humor is really displaced anger, a social weapon used by those who want to dominate and pull strings. It certainly can remove inhibitions and destroy "out-of-date" taboos (whether they are good or not).[4] Humor has even been used in wartime to undermine the morale of the enemy. But perhaps the strongest influence of comedy can be found in its social control. Humor can be used as punishment, can arouse fear, and can effectively keep a person from straying from group values.[5] It is especially effective in keeping *young* people inside group norms.

The message in much of today's comedy is obvious if you watch television. It comes across anti-establishment and makes adults look like incompetents; or worse, dumb is shown to be cool, and the working class is glamorized.[6]

These messages become even more powerful when mass media comes into the picture. By sweetening the sitcoms with a laugh track, the producers "tell" us what is funny (e.g. violence). They also tell us what is not funny by leaving the laugh track out. We have noticed a disturbing trend as mass media powerbrokers join with comedians to direct our path in comedy. More and more jokes are becoming suggestive, sacrilegious, and even vicious.

In the past few years, ministers and television evangelists have come under increasing attack from the so-called comedy of the mass media. When you begin to laugh at someone with the intention of humiliation, that humor is being used as a weapon, and it's as sharp as a sword. When the laugh tracks tell us over and over again that laughing at this kind of "violence" is okay, gradually our guard is let down, and we find ourselves laughing at things that would have once brought righteous indignation.

Science Digest described this approach to humor in an article, "Fun, As In Funeral." The author commented that comedy is becoming more sinister, hostile, and cruel.[7] Another publication talked about how humor is even being pulled from tragedy.[8] What once was sick and tragic is now an object of laughter.

This power of ridicule and aggressive comedy should not be underestimated. Many of our most treasured and sacred family values will be shattered and uprooted if we let young, impressionable minds be subjected to the subliminal manipulation of so-called "black comedy." Guard your family, and don't neglect to watch out for this kind of humor—for wolves can even come in comedian's clothing.

Chapter 13

FILM-BROKERS

The last aspect of the mass media we will cover is the film industry. Specifically, we want to alert Christians of all ages to alarming developments in the current film experience. Everything we have discussed in previous chapters relates to movies. Films serve as trendsetters, provide role models, contain subliminal messages, and are controlled by people you may not want influencing your children.

Messages of promiscuity, drug abuse, violence, rebellion, and other undesirable values are transmitted through certain films just like they are in television, rock music, comedy, and subliminal advertising. There is, however, a dangerous development in popular movies that you will definitely want to know about. This unique message may be preparing your child for the most disastrous event in his or her life.

The danger comes from "certain mythic, archetypal images once communicated in Christian art, but now assuming a non-Christian form, which are *submerged beneath the surface meanings* of works bearing the immediate appearances of ordinary reality or various styles of 'fantasy.' "[1] More and more popular movies are teaching our society religious messages that were once reserved for the Church, and the kids are eating it up!

Most parents with small children already know the impact movies have, for their kids can tell them amazingly correct details about *Star Wars* or *The Return Of The Jedi*. Not only do they remember even the smallest detail, chances are they have managed to obtain various pieces of paraphernalia concerning their favorite movie. Lunch boxes, miniature figures, lighted swords, coloring books, model spaceships, and countless other products keep the message fresh in your child's mind. Let's look at the messages invading our children's lives.

Oscar-winning writer Frank Tarloff said, "So much of the philosophy of young people arises from what they see in movies and on television. That's where they acquire much of their mores. A steady diet of distortion of life can lead to unrealistic expectations."[2] The director of *Return Of The Jedi,* Irvin Kershner, added, "What we now have is a psychic depression. That's why so many people are turning to religion. They want to believe in God."[3] Do you see the dangerous situation developing? There is a great hunger for spiritual experiences among our children, and films are providing the images that were once communicated in Christian art.

Religious, supernatural themes have become common in many of the most popular movies of our day. *Superman* featured a higher intelligence from the heavens who sent his only son to earth. The son then became the central figure in the fight against evil. *Star Wars* bears a remarkable resemblance to Ephesians 6 in the Bible. *Close Encounters* features a "descent of gods." Hell images are invoked in *Jaws* and *Invasion Of The Body Snatchers*. *Gremlins* featured little devilish creatures who terrorize an entire community. The word "gremlin" means *demon*.

One of the most striking examples occurs in the incredibly popular film, *E.T.* This influential little character descended from the heavens, had light within himself, healed by the laying on of hands, possessed a young boy by joining personality and soul with him, died and returned to life, and ascended home. Before departing, E.T. touched the young boy's heart and said, "I'll be right here."[4]

If you still have doubts about the religious influence of films, perhaps this quote from *USA Today* will change your mind: "This capacity to stir the imagination is an element that many people find missing in modern Christianity, shorn as it is of cosmic and supernatural dimensions. In this regard, the films of such artists as George Lucas and Steven Spielberg feed a developing surrogate religious consciousness that looks to the film experience, rather than the cathedral, for soul-stirring integration."[5]

In other words, films are giving our kids a new religion that in turn affects *every area* of their life. The main message behind this new "religion" is one of the most dangerous and potentially disastrous influences in our children's lives.

As in much of today's music, the main danger in this film message is the preparation of our young people to receive supernatural visitations and experiences. Think about the themes of the movies your kids watch. How many times is the grotesque alien initially rejected, only to turn out as friendly and benevolent? Movie after movie tells us that we only need to understand these visitors; they really mean us no harm. If you are a Christian, you certainly don't want your children to be conditioned to openly receive gremlins (demons) or spiritual visitors.

The Bible predicts increased supernatural and demonic activity in the time just before the return of Christ. If, as many Bible scholars believe, we are approaching that time, the last thing our kids need to be taught is to accept the evil side of the supernatural. They should be warned of the danger, not taught to become friends with strange alien beings with spiritual powers. In foretelling the return of Jesus, 2 Thessalonians 2:9-11 warns us that Satan will work with power, signs, and lying wonders, deceiving many. The world will believe the lie.

Many of today's films are preparing a new generation to readily receive these deceptive signs and lying wonders. Stephen Spielberg, in commenting on *Close Encounters* and *Poltergeist,* said, "One element of the movie is when the youngest child in the house is abducted by an unseen consciousness that holds her for emotional ransom for quite a long while. . . . I think it's very spiritual."[6] Christians will recognize "abduction by an unseen consciousness" as true demonic oppression.

As a young girl, Irene Park was visited by a spiritual creature who eventually befriended her and became her "guide." The adults thought it was cute that Irene had an "imaginary" friend. Unfortunately, the visitation was not imagined, as the rest of Irene's life proved. From this one encounter with the supernatural, she was eventually drawn into the occult with all her energy. She became one of the most influential satanists in the country; but, just as Satan was destroying her, she found new life in Christ and became *The Witch That Switched*. Her book vividly warns against playing with the occult.

Don't let anyone in your family think it is all right to dabble with supernatural manifestations outside of the Lord Jesus Christ. If your child is visited by a creature resembling *E.T.,* don't let him think he should hide it in the closet and protect it from the misinformed adults who just "don't understand." And, certainly, he should never let anything possess him or "join" his mind.

Chapter 14

MANIPULATING THE MANIPULATORS

One of the reasons I wrote this book on subliminal messages in mass media is because of the Church's lack of knowledge in this area. We have a choice in partaking of such immoralities as pornography and vulgarity when we know about them. If the messages are hidden, it takes away our free will—our right to choose. The subliminal messages in media have gone beyond attacking our values and traditions. Media has stepped into parental, educational, and religious roles. For better or worse, mass media is right in the middle of the end-time destiny for planet Earth. We believe the evidence indicates that the media has overwhelmingly been on one side of the battle for the souls of men.

Before I go on to suggest answers to the problems of media manipulation, I would like to make it clear that I am assuming the readers of this book are Christians. The answers I will give apply only to those who have been born again. If you would like to know more about why you should become a Christian and how you can be born again, please turn to Appendix II in the back of this book. Now, for those who are still with me, and for you who have just now joined the family, let us push on into the *reality* behind subliminal manipulation in mass media.

There are at least four major reasons mass media's hidden agenda reveals a sinister source. Evidence indicates that the mass media has been (perhaps unwittingly) used as a tool for satanic infiltration into our society and our family. Some people have a remarkable ability to sense trouble. They can "smell a rat" at all times, even before all the facts are in. While some people have this special ability, everyone knows a rat when they *see* one. If it looks like a rat, runs like a rat, smells like a rat, and eats like a rat, there is a good chance it *is* a rat.

Let's compare subliminal manipulation to demonic activity and see how closely they relate. The first area of similarity is in the techniques used to accomplish their goals. Recently I listened to a sermon on deliverance and demonology in which the minister gave sure ways to spot demon activity. Deception is the devil's number one tool. He is the father of all lies. (See John 8:44.) Subliminal seduction is also based on deception. In fact, if a person recognizes the truth, the technique doesn't work. It is based *entirely* on manipulation and deception.

Another characteristic of demonic influence is compulsion—being driven to do something even if it is against your will. Subliminal messages also seek to compel you to act in a way you would not ordinarily act. Addiction and uncontrollable desires work well for the marketer. Deception, manipulation, and the creation of uncontrollable desires are all common in both camps.

A second connection is the values and beliefs of both demons and subliminal manipulators. To a large extent they believe and value the same things. As we saw in Chapter 4, the people controlling the mass media hold values that make them natural enemies of fundamentalist Christian groups like the Moral Majority. They are pro-homosexual, favor free sex, advocate abortion on demand, and are generally anti-establishment. Demons would say a hearty "amen" to all of these beliefs.

In addition to their values, the *messages* each give are remarkably similar. What is the nature of messages that encourage housewives to buy irrationally and impulsively or that play on hidden weaknesses and frailties? What is the morality in manipulating small children, exploiting sexual sensitivities, treating voters like customers, planning product obsolescence, arousing deep emotions such as hate, envy, and fear, or manipulating human personality by invading the privacy of the mind?[1]

Ernest Dichter, one of the founders of consumer motivational research, said, "The problem of morality has to be approached in a scientific fashion rather than a theological one."[2] He goes on to say that a key for marketing success is the ability to relieve the guilt in consumers. This offer of absolution outside of the Word of God goes right back to the original message of Satan in the Garden of Eden. Even then, he was saying, "Ye shall not surely die" (Genesis 3:4).

Finally, in addition to the techniques, values, and messages, the *fruit* of the media and demonic manipulation is identical. People have been freed from "out-of-date" inhibitions, but the price has been great. Divorce is now commonplace, affecting half of all marriages in our nation. Abortion slaughters multiplied *millions* of innocent babies. Homosexuality is spreading like a plague, bringing AIDS into the blood supply of mainstream America. Drug abuse, alcoholism, crime, pornography, child abuse, teenage suicide, gambling, corruption, sexual promiscuity, adultery, homosexuality, rebellion, and confusion have all led to the breakdown of our family institution.

When the family falls, our entire nation cannot help but be affected. The point is not to dwell on tragedy. We simply want to make it clear that the results of subliminal messages in mass media are identical to the results of following the "god of this world." (See 2 Corinthians 4:4.)

Many excellent organizations have dedicated themselves to the struggle of correcting the institutions being used by Satan. We support and strongly encourage your participation in these worthy efforts. These organizations range from anti-pornography fighters to protectors of religious liberty. These are important works, and we stand be-

95

hind the courageous efforts to return the institutions of our country to a biblically-based morality. Pray and support these groups in any way you can. If you are being called into a specific area or would like more information, we have enclosed a special list of ministries, legal efforts, and more detailed exposes in certain areas, such as music. (See Appendix III.)

While the struggle for social change is certainly needed, our main purpose is to help individuals and families overcome personal difficulties in the home. The Lord has given us answers to help you overcome the assault in your own life. As we have seen in this chapter, the true enemy is a spiritual one and must be dealt with in a spiritual battle. We assume that you already believe in the spirit-world. Settle this point because all the fighting skills in the world won't do a bit of good if you don't know who to fight.

"Therefore I do not run uncertainly—without definite aim. I do not box as one beating the air and striking without an adversary" (1 Corinthians 9:26, *Amplified*).

"For we are not wrestling with flesh and blood— contending only with physical opponents—but against the despotisms, against the powers, against [the master spirits who are] the world rulers of this present darkness, against the spirit forces of wickedness in the heavenly (supernatural) sphere" (Ephesians 6:12, *Amplified*).

The last chapter of this book deals with solutions to the problems that so easily beset us. Because the answer lies in the spiritual realm, we will begin focusing on the supernatural as it relates to our daily lives.

Chapter 15

THE ANSWER

If you have been reading this book to find answers to some of the problems facing you or your children, this chapter lays down effective and proven ways to deal with the difficulties. In fact, I contend that following these guidelines is the only way to keep one's head above water in these turbulent times. It may not be what you want to hear, and it may not agree with your theology or upbringing. Just do one thing: Instead of leaning on your feelings or understanding, ask God to reveal to you what He wants you to know. Only receive what the Holy Spirit makes real to your spirit. Then let it flow to your mind and renew it according to God's will.

One of the major mistakes parents and churches make in dealing with young people is *catering to their culture*. The youth of today are not looking for more "cool" people. They want answers! Regardless of the way a youth leader dresses or talks, if he or she does not have the power of the Holy Spirit working through his life, it is all futile. Again, in dealing with your children, you don't have to try and be "with it." At best, this usually is just a mockery in their eyes and will subconsciously be viewed as compromise.

On the other hand, don't try to make them adopt your "culture." This is just as bad as trying to adopt theirs. The way to true communion and fellowship among the members of your family is not along the road of compromise or conformity. It is not a question of social custom or personal preference. It is a spiritual problem, and it will take spiritual answers. Remember, we are spiritual beings in a spiritually influenced world. Unless we get into the *real world* and do battle, we will lose by default. There is no choice in the matter. The devil is not asking for a vote. He is determined to destroy you and your loved ones and will stop at nothing within his reach to accomplish that goal.

Don't offer feeble attempts at what you think your children want to hear. Always offer an alternative—a choice for radical commitment. When the time is right and your children are ready to make decisions for Christ, you better have been consistent in offering them a deep, life-changing alternative. The first step in overcoming the wickedness of this world is to make a *radical commitment* to Christ. It means giving *all* to Him.

Don't be deceived by religious men who simply tell you to agree mentally with the facts of the Bible. It takes more than that. Demons believe intellectually and tremble. (See James 2:19.) It takes giving your whole life to Him—radical commitment. Don't take anyone's opinion in this matter. The stakes are too high. Read in Mark 10:21 where Jesus told the rich young ruler to go and sell all that he had. Read where Jesus said, "If any man will come after me, let him deny himself, and take up his cross, and follow me" (Matthew 16:24).

This should not be interpreted to mean we must do this or that to become saved. Ephesians 2:8-9 says quite clearly that we are saved by God's grace through our faith. It is a gift of God, not a result of our works.

What then was Jesus talking about when He said to give all that we had? He means giving the most important thing of all: *ourselves.* Commitment means giving our life to Him, being willing to do what He tells us to do—not what we think is right or what we feel like doing. It is a matter of who is Lord of our life. Will we allow Jesus to be the Savior and *Lord* of our lives, or will we insist on being our own lord? This fundamental question must be made clear to all those who find themselves overcome by the wiles of the devil.

There is a choice to make, but it involves surrender. It involves a total, radical commitment to let God run our lives. This decision means living Proverbs 3:5-6: "Trust in the Lord with all thine heart; and lean not unto thine own understanding. In all thy ways acknowledge him, and he shall direct thy paths."

Once this decision is made, it is very important

to continue to try to be led by the Spirit of God. We are to continue in the Lord in the same way we receive Him. (See Colossians 2:6.) When we are born again, the foundation is laid. Now we need to let the Master builder follow His blueprint—the destiny He has for our lives—and build us into that perfect part of the body of Christ that only we can be. If we try to build ourselves into something, we won't fit. He has created us unto certain works. Each of us has a special destiny and function to fulfill. But unless we are obedient to the Spirit, God won't have the liberty to bring us into all He has planned. We ourselves will limit Him.

Parents, are you willing to give your kids into God's hands? Do you really trust Him? What if it means that your kids won't "fit in" anymore? They may seem like fools to the rest of the world. In fact, Jesus declared that we should not be surprised if the world *hates us*. It hated Him, and we as His servants are not greater than our Lord.

After becoming alive spiritually and making the commitment to be led spiritually, the next step in victorious living is to be endowed with power. Jesus breathed on the disciples in the upper room, and they received the Holy Spirit. They were born again, became new creatures, and were made alive spiritually. But they were then commanded to remain until they would be baptized with power. They already had the Spirit *in* them but needed the power of the Spirit *on* them. This happened in the second chapter of Acts, when the disciples received the baptism of the Holy Spirit and spoke with other tongues. (See John 4:24 and Acts 2.) These men were already born again, but the miracles did not occur until after they were endowed with this special anointing.

In these end times, it is absolutely essential that we receive *everything* God has for us. We must be fully equipped, not in order to be saved but to fight the good fight of faith. You can lay hold on "the promised land" for yourself and your family. In a supernatural world, the only way to victory is through the supernatural. Jesus walked in it, and the early Christians walked in it. We also should walk in it.

If you have not received the baptism in the Holy Spirit and would like to, you can do so right now. In childlike trust go to the Father, and in Jesus' name ask for this baptism with His power. Do you want to be an effective witness? Do you want to be obedient? This anointing will help you receive the strength to do just that. Begin to worship and praise Him from your innermost being. Let His praises flow from your lips, and give Him thanks for baptizing you in the Holy Spirit. Never give up on your quest for the fullness of God's Spirit! "Seek, and ye shall find, knock, and it shall be opened unto you" (Matthew 7:7).

Strength For The Inner Man

You may already be a saved, Spirit-filled Christian, but you know there is more to the Christian life than you are experiencing. Too many things have you bound: bad habits, fears, peer pressure, lack of faith, sexual lusts, etc. Or perhaps you simply want more of the supernatural. Maybe there are too many problems you do not have the answers for, and you want to be able to help those people with desperate needs—physical, spiritual, mental, or even financial.

The problem may be that the supernatural is not your normal life. A miracle may be experienced now and then, but it is the exception rather than the rule. This is the problem with countless believers today. They want to be everything God wants them to be, but they just can't seem to get out of the rut they are in.

Preachers have taught that to overcome we must study the Word, witness for the Lord, attend church, and fellowship with other believers. This, they say, will give us faith and lead us into the abundant life. Unfortunately, for many Christians the Bible is dry and puts them to sleep. This in turn leads to feelings of guilt, for the devil is ever ready to pounce on Christians with accusations. (See Revelation 12:10.)

Is your witness inhibited by an overwhelming fear that prohibits you from carrying out what you know you should do? Perhaps a bad habit has you in chains. Sins of the flesh may time and time again lead you into defeat. You want to give these things up, but somehow you can't. Trying to do the "right things," such as reading the Word and witnessing, only leads to more frustration, boredom, and guilt. Have you ever found yourself in this situation?

A stock "answer" is that you only have to "die to self." That sounds great, but try to ask someone exactly how you go about dying to self! We all have a strong temptation to heap teachers to scratch our itching ears. We leave services talking about how blessed the preaching was, but are we really any different after we leave?

The concept of dying to self certainly has a biblical basis. The trouble is that we can focus on saying "no" to our fleshly desires but never accomplish anything for eternity. Paul describes this type of religious activity in Colossians 2:20-23. He says these ordinances such as touch not, taste not, and handle not do have a show of wisdom in will-worship and neglecting the body. Do you want to worship your willpower or the risen Lord? Paul goes on to state that we should "seek those things which are above, where Christ sitteth on the right hand of God" (Colossians 3:1).

Before going on, I should mention that if you are selling some brand of self-neglect through willpower, you might as well forget about helping your kids. Too many forces tempt their flesh for this to work. It takes something much more convincing than the philosophy of self-restraint to keep them walking with the Lord.

What is the answer? It is close to what you may have heard, but there is one crucial difference. Instead of doing all types of Christian activities to get close to the Lord, you should come into the presence of God *first*, then go out and do His works by His leading. Don't read the Bible to get close to God. Come to Him in prayerful and thankful submission. Ask Him to enlighten the Scriptures to you, for you are completely submitted and surrendered to His will. You will be amazed at how different the Bible will become! Instead of a boring lesson in religion, it will become the living, active Word. Again, read the Word because you *are* close to God, not in order to *get* close to Him.

Turn back to Proverbs 3:5-6. Make this the foundation for governing your life. In everything, come to God first in surrender and worship. This will lead to the anointing of the Holy Spirit in all you do. If you are led by the Spirit in reading the Bible, it will be alive. If the Holy Spirit wants you to talk to someone about the Lord, anointing will be there. The key is to let Him lead. Jesus Himself said He never did anything unless He saw the Father do it. He was led by the Spirit one-hundred percent of the time. (See John 5:19.)

An illustration of the way we have been turned around in our thinking is clear in the sermons we have heard on Romans 10:17: "Faith cometh by hearing, and hearing by the word of God." This verse is often used to prove that if we only read the Bible long enough our faith will surely rise, elevating us into the victory we desire.

A closer examination of the verse, however, reveals something different than what you may have heard. The Greek translation of "word" is *rhema*. Whenever you see "word" in the New Testament, it stems from one of two root words: *rhema* or *logos*. Simply stated, logos means the declared law of God that never changes. You could look at the written word (the Bible) as being logos. Rhema is used to identify those logos (written words) which are made alive by the Spirit of God. When they are quickened by the Spirit, these words become incredibly powerful in changing the world. Without that quickening, we can easily be caught up in well-meaning but dead works.

The basic idea is that we must come to God *first*. We must rely on His strength and leading in *everything* we do, from reading the Bible to preaching a sermon. This makes the Christian life unattractive to many. You must surrender the throne of your life and let Jesus be your *Lord,* not just a convenience to be used when the need arises.

Do you want to know how to "die to self"? The key is being led by the Holy Spirit in *every area* of your life. If you are doing what God is telling you to do, the flesh is automatically denied. The more you are led by the Holy Spirit, the more your flesh will lose its power over you.

Once the conclusion is reached to be led by God and not yourself, several more questions must be asked: "How can I be led by the Spirit? How can I tell the voice of God? Is it me or the devil talking? How do you tell the difference?"

Overcoming In This Life

You must learn to distinguish between at least three voices—the Holy Spirit, your own thinking or feeling, and evil spirits. Every decision in life is a choice from among these voices. You must follow one or the other. If you want the help you are looking for in overcoming life's problems, the Holy Spirit must be followed.

Mind manipulation may give apparent results, but you don't just want the outside action to look right. Actions must be motivated correctly from the heart to mean anything, for the Lord weighs the heart, discerning thoughts and intentions. (See Hebrews 4:12.) You may get yourself or your child to act right out of sheer willpower or dominance; but, in the end, this method won't stand before God. It also won't stand once your child is faced with a life-changing decision that he must make alone.

We have seen how the devil works on the mind, trying to implant fears, inadequacies, and lusts. He tempts the flesh and entices the mind with every conceivable lie and deception. In today's world we are bombarded on every side by temptation. If we go into a store, we must look at filthy porno magazines or nude and suggestive advertisements all over the shelf. Every type of psychological device is used to trick us into making a purchase of something we neither need nor want.

The nightly news fills the air with liberal and humanistic coverage. Our schools are training grounds for humanists where teachers try to strip away the morality we teach our children. Films consistently portray Christians as buffoons or weird killers. Books, popular music, peer pressure—all create an overwhelming avalanche of ungodliness that almost sweeps us away.

Now can you better understand why your children may be behaving in ways that oppose the morals you have taught them? Parents, wake up! The forces that have arisen against today's youth are incredibly strong. Mere talk will not help. At one time our society may have "allowed" us to live out quiet religious lives, but the day is over! These are the end times. And, as the Bible warns, evil men will grow worse and worse, deceiving and being deceived. (See 2 Timothy 3:13.) Like it or not, we are living in the last days.

Only one solution exists for the problems we face, and it is *not* to be removed from the circumstances. The Bible predicts that things will get worse, not better, in the world system. (See 1 John 2:18.) We can't leave the situation. The answer is to live exactly like Jesus lived. He existed in a realm that gave Him victory in every situation. *Nothing ever happened to Jesus that defeated Him.* Death tried. Disease tried. The devil tried, again and again. Jesus overcame them all! How? He lived in the Spirit. Jesus knew instantly who was speaking to Him.

Strong voices rule the average individual. Our

flesh demands certain things, and our emotions pull toward others. Another voice is our understanding or logic. Buried deep within these bold and loud urgings is a still, small voice. At this innermost place of your being—the spirit or heart—God is heard. Jesus said those who worship God *must* worship Him in spirit and in truth. (See John 4:24.) You may have been trying to follow God or worship Him with your mind or your feelings. He commands us to be led by His Spirit and not by our own understanding. (See Proverbs 3:5-6.)

One school of thought centers on rejecting the urging of the flesh and the mind. We are supposed to become more like Christ if we don't do certain things. I contend that it is not what we *don't do* that makes us more like Jesus, but it is what we *do* in a positive way. Specifically, to be led by the Spirit, don't try to beat your flesh or your mind into submission. If your spirit has not become strong enough to take over the ground the flesh or mind has given up, it will become desolate, and "beasts of the field will multiply against thee" (Exodus 23:29).

Our walk into the overcoming life parallels the children of Israel's fight to take over the promised land. They took one city at a time as they became strong enough and *as the Lord led them*. God warned them that He would direct them and give them the victory if they would trust Him and heed His voice.

As our spirit grows in strength, it will begin to take over the land. The enemies of our spiritual development can be walled cities in our mind—fears, hurts, bitterness, etc. These strongholds must be cast down because they hinder our victory and cause us to stop short of the answer to our prayer. They make the Word less effective. These negative areas are Satan's foothold in our life and are being manipulated by an ungodly world system.

Our spirit will become stronger when it is used. When we worship God in spirit, when we are led by the Holy Spirit, and when we allow God to use us (through our spirits) for miracles or healings, our spirit takes its rightful place at the control of our lives. The key is to build up the spirit. "Walk in the Spirit, and ye shall not fulfill the lust of the flesh" (Galatians 5:16).

All the negative areas in our lives will be taken care of when we learn to walk in the power and anointing of the Spirit. The answer to your child's difficulties is not found in simply overpowering his fleshly desires with your fleshly desires (no matter how "good" they might seem). The answer is to give yourself and your family over into the hands of a supernatural, miracle-working God. Your child may not be impressed by your "with it" gospel message; but show him the power of the Almighty God by delivering a demon-possessed person, and you can be assured of his interest and deep respect. No one wants words and opinions anymore. The reality of the gospel must be demonstrated in power and holiness. This is the way to overcome in this age.

We must learn to hear and follow the voice of the

Spirit of God so we can be victorious. One way to develop this "ear" to hear is to pray in tongues. This builds up your spirit while bypassing your mind. (See 1 Corinthians 14:2,4; Jude 20.) Pray often. Pray for hours, days, weeks, and months. Expect to feel *worse* at first. The mind and flesh will be losing their places of control in your life, and they will not go down quietly. The flesh will scream for attention. The mind will want to quit. Keep praying in tongues. This is something you can do any time. It is a gift from God. Use it.

When you pray in tongues for extended periods of time, you will begin to discern quiet leadings coming from deep inside your spirit that you have never heard before. Follow these leadings. Remember, God speaks through your spirit, not your mind or feelings. Our minds and feelings are supposed to be controlled by our spirits, not vice-versa.

As you begin to follow your spirit, you will learn to distinguish His voice. At times you may miss God. Don't give up! We are trained to hear His voice above all others by following Him again and again. (See Romans 8:14.)

Begin with the smallest things. Ask God what to wear in the morning. Talk to Him like He's there (He is!). Ask when to do certain activities, and then ask His anointing on them after He guides you to do it. That activity will instantly take on a new dimension. The anointing of the Spirit of God will flow through your life when you do *His* will instead of your own. Don't ask God to bless something you cook up. Let *Him* do the leading. He has the destiny for your life. He created you to be something special, and only He knows how to bring us to that fullness. He has the blueprint—let Him do the building.

The sparks that grow into the flame of the spirit-filled life are praying in tongues and being led by the Holy Spirit. Tongues build up your spirit so you can become sensitive to the voice of the Holy Spirit.

Once you begin to hear the Holy Spirit's voice, follow it. The mind and the flesh (as influenced by the devil) may prevent you from following the leading of God in certain situations. Don't give up! Repent, tell it to God, and He will cleanse you from all unrighteousness. Then determine more than ever that at some point (just around the corner), you *will* obey the Spirit in that area. Every day you are growing stronger in your spirit, and some day soon the spirit will overtake the flesh or the mind in that weak area—victory will be yours to the glory of the Father!

Keep growing in obedience to the Spirit, and God will begin doing fantastic things in your life. This is the life you have wanted. It is the abundant life God wants for you. He is ready and willing. All He needs is a people who will be led by their spirit (God's point of contact with us) and not by their flesh.

Should we read the Bible? Yes! Should we witness and fellowship? Yes! We should do all the Christian activities such as attending church and tithing, but do so when, where, and how God leads you. Let Him put His anointing on what would have been dead religious works. Humble yourself in the sight of God, and He will exalt you in due time. (See 1 Peter 5:6.)

How can we overcome the effects of subliminal manipulation in our lives? By submitting to the leading of the Holy Spirit, we become overcomers in this life. Not only does this free us now but Jesus said to those that overcome:

"I will give to eat of the tree of life, which is in the midst of the paradise of God. He shall not be hurt of the second death. I will give to eat of the hidden manna. I will give power over nations. I will give him the morning star. The same shall be clothed in white raiment; and I will not blot out his name out of the book of life, but will confess his name before my Father, and before his angels. I will make him a pillar in the temple of my God. To him that overcometh will I grant to sit with me in my throne, even as I also overcame, and am set down with my Father in his throne" (Revelation 2:7-3:21).

SUMMARY

In order to be freed from the manipulation of subliminal messages and the influence of the world system, we must walk in the supernatural. If we walk in the Spirit, we will not fulfill the lust of the flesh. (See Galatians 5:16.) Subliminal manipulation is designed to feed our flesh. If the technique is recognized, it can be stopped from affecting us by our conscious guard (i.e. morals, values, etc.). This is the first step toward freedom from the bondage of the world system. Become an expert in detecting subliminal messages all around you. When the message is recognized, it loses its power to influence you subconsciously. In other words, quit feeding the flesh—stop its food supply!

On the other hand, learn to feed your spirit. This is done by praying in the spirit (tongues) and being led by the Holy Spirit in all you do, such as reading the Bible, witnessing, etc. When the flesh is starved and the spirit is fed, we enter deeper and deeper into the supernatural Christian life. This is the key to overcoming.

When we learn to live in the Spirit, abide in the Vine, and walk in the Light, we will crush the devil and all his subliminal seduction under our feet.

Appendix I

OTHER SUBLIMINAL INFLUENCES

Although our study has focused primarily on subliminal messages in mass media, other groups with similar goals influence our families. In an effort to "guard our hearts" and be victorious over the schemes of the devil, we must recognize all possible sources of subtle manipulation. Let's take a look at a few contemporary organizations involved in a battle perhaps greater than they realize.

New Age Movement

The New Age Movement is a worldwide effort of various organizations to bring about a new world order. Their goals include one-world food distribution, one-world money (supply based on a cashless system), one-world religion, one international armed service, number assignment of each individual, and one-world government to be headed by an emerging leader.[1]

In 1982, full-page ads ran in major newspapers

around the world announcing that "The Christ Is Now Here." These ads were run by New Age organizations that believe the new world leader (or Christ) is now ready to assume leadership of the earth. The ad stated:

"THE WORLD HAS HAD ENOUGH . . . OF HUNGER, INJUSTICE, WAR. IN ANSWER TO OUR CALL FOR HELP, AS WORLD TEACHER FOR ALL HUMANITY—THE CHRIST IS NOW HERE.

"HOW WILL WE RECOGNIZE HIM?

"Look for a modern man concerned with modern problems—political, economic, and social. Since July 1977, the Christ has been emerging as a spokesman for a group or community in a well-known modern country. He is not a religious leader, but an educator in the broadest sense of the word—pointing the way out of our present crisis. We will recognize Him by His extraordinary spiritual potency, the universality of His viewpoint, and His love for all humanity. He comes not to judge, but to aid and inspire.

"WHO IS THE CHRIST?

"Throughout history, humanity's evolution has been guided by a group of enlightened men, the Masters of Wisdom. They have remained largely in the remote desert and mountain places of earth, working mainly through their disciples who live openly in the world. This message of the Christ's reappearance has been given primarily by such a disciple trained for his task for over 20 years. At the

117

center of this 'Spiritual Hierarchy' stands the World Teacher, LORD MAITREYA, known by Christians as the CHRIST. And as Christians await the Second Coming, so the Jew awaits the MESSIAH, the Buddhist the FIFTH BUDDA, the Moslem the IMAM MAHDI, and the Hindus await KRISHNA. These are all names for one individual. His presence in the world guarantees there will be no third World War.

"WHAT IS HE SAYING?

" 'My task will be to show you how to live together peacefully as brothers. This is simpler than you imagine, My friends, for it requires only the acceptance of sharing.

" 'How can you be content with the modes within which you now live; when millions starve and die in squalor; when the rich parade their wealth before the poor; when each man is his neighbor's enemy; when no man trusts his brother?

" 'Allow me to show you the way forward into the simpler life where no man lacks; where no two days are alike; were the Joy of Brotherhood manifests through all men.

" 'Take your brother's need as the measure for your action and solve the problems of the world.'

"WHEN WILL WE SEE HIM?

"He has not as yet declared His true status, and His location is known to only a very few disciples. One of these has announced that soon the Christ will acknowledge His identity and within the next two months will speak to humanity through a worldwide television and radio broadcast. His message will be

118

heard inwardly, telepathically, by all people in their own language. From that time, with His help, we will begin to build a new world.

"WITHOUT SHARING THERE CAN BE NO JUSTICE.

"WITHOUT JUSTICE THERE CAN BE NO PEACE.

"WITHOUT PEACE THERE CAN BE NO FUTURE.

"This ad is appearing simultaneously in major cities of the world."

What this full page ad did not tell the unsuspecting reader is that the roots of the movement can be traced to the occultic writings of Alice Bailey and Helen Blavatsky. These two women were instrumental in laying the framework for this New Age Movement and even gave specific directions on bringing the movement into power. Helen Blavatsky wrote about telepathic communication and psychic phenomena, claimed to be enlightened by masters or spirit guides, advocated the merging of all the world's religions, and was openly hostile toward orthodox Christianity.

Alice Bailey's work was published by Lucifer Publishing Company. She advocated redistribution of the world's resources, one-world religion, unilateral disarmament, mystical experiences (including enlightenment by "masters"), Luciferic initiations, and evolution involving higher races. She even stated the sacredness of the number 666. Her directions were to remain secret until 1982, when the movement was to go public. As we have stated, this was

119

the very year the ads ran around the world.

Alarmingly, many naive but well-meaning people are supporting this movement without realizing the goals and philosophy behind it. Some organizations pushing toward a one-world food distribution system have members who are genuinely concerned about hunger in the world. Little do they know that the very movement they are supporting will one day require total allegiance to a world leader or they will give you *no* food.

Beware of any organization advocating a one-world system to end the earth's problems. Only one true peace and only one answer exists—Jesus Christ of Nazareth.

The Occult

Evil carries a certain attractiveness. It offers temporary pleasure and power. One of the favorite devices of the occult is luring people into its ranks by offering free sex and an abundance of drugs. Another deception is the power that is available. A witch thinks she is controlling the spirits; but in the end, she will find out (as former witch Irene Park discovered) that the devil uses people for his own destructive purposes. When he is through, he will take great pleasure in killing you. There are no white witches and black witches. Any contact with the spirit world outside of the guidance and power of the Holy Spirit is very dangerous.[2]

Transcendental meditation, yoga, psychic phenomena, satanic worship, new age enlightenment, out-of-body experiences, and even much of science fiction is nothing but another twist to the age-old deception used by Satan throughout the history of man. Films today are encouraging contact with alien beings—i.e., *ET*, the blockbuster movie, involved an alien space being and a young boy. ET died and came back to life, healed by the laying on of hands, merged souls with the boy, and clearly opened the way for young people to readily accept contact with alien spirits.

Witches and satanic priests who have been saved and delivered have personally warned me about the dangers in these popular movies. Many of the characters such as the Gremlins are truly representative of demons. Beware of the influence of the occult in all areas of our society. Remember, Satan comes frequently as an angel of light. (See 2 Corinthians 11:14.)

NEA And Humanism

The National Education Association represents 1.7 million teachers. The President of the NEA predicted in 1967 that the "NEA will become a political power unmatched by any other organized group." We have lived to witness that day. With such political power and almost total control over our public schools, it is important to understand the philosophy and goals of this powerful organization.[3]

John Dewey was instrumental in formulating the

social goals for our public educational system. The NEA has followed the basic social guidelines of John Dewey for years. Dewey, a confirmed socialist and humanist, wrote that social planning (by public education) is the method by which liberalism can reach its aims. He advocated an entire educational system that prepares citizens for a socialist, amoral society.

Dewey helped pen the *Humanist Manifesto I,* which stated that "the universe is self-existing and not created . . . that the complete realization of human personality is the end of man's life . . . and that Man is at last becoming aware that he alone is responsible for the realization of the world of his dreams, that he has within himself the power for its achievement . . . that the nature of the universe depicted by modern science makes unacceptable any supernatural or cosmic guarantees of human values."[4]

An updated *Humanist Manifesto* was published in 1973. It stated:

"As in 1933, humanists still believe that traditional theism, especially faith in the prayer-hearing God . . . is an unproven and outmoded faith. Salvationism, based on mere affirmation, still appears as harmful, diverting people with false hopes of heaven hereafter.

"The next century can be and should be the humanist century. . . . We can control our environment, conquer poverty, markedly reduce disease, extend our life-span, significantly modify our behaviour, alter the course of human evolution and cultural development, and unlock vast new powers. . . .

"We affirm a set of common principles that can serve as a basis for united action. . . . They are a design for a secular society on a planetary scale."

The *Humanist Manifesto II* goes on to state, "No diety will save us; we must save ourselves." Among the signers of this document are Betty Friedan, founder of the National Organization of Women, Alan F. Guttmacher, president of Planned Parenthood, and Lester Mondale (related to and supported by Walter Mondale), former president of the Fellowship of Religious Humanists.

Has the NEA adapted this humanistic and socialistic agenda for our public school system? Today, the NEA's goals include gun control, abortion on demand, values clarification, situational ethics, sex education, nuclear freeze, marxist revolution in Central America, disarmament, the Equal Rights Amendment, and evolutionary humanistic values. The NEA opposes voluntary school prayer, U.S. aid for anticommunist fighters in Central America, and competency testing for teachers. The organization is increasingly hostile toward Christians and other conservative groups.

With this in mind, consider the danger of the NEA's 1976 "declaration of independence" and "education for the global community." Are these the people we want clarifying the values we teach our children?

Computerized Economic Control

Another development you should watch closely involves the electronic, computerized takeover of financial transactions. The Universal Product Code and its marks, which can be seen on virtually all merchandise, has been broken down to the numerical code 666. If you will recall, the book of Revelation says that in the end-time people will be required to receive a *mark,* not necessarily a number, in order to buy and sell.

Currently, in many parts of the country, cards are being issued that have necessary personal information recorded on marks in the black magnetic strip. You've probably noticed these on the back of your credit cards. With this latest technology, all you need is your card (complete with encoded "mark") to buy and sell. A teller will plug your card into the terminal, and the amount of the purchase will automatically be transferred from your savings account to the store's account.[5]

When we first read about these developments, it was hard to believe that such a system could already be in practice. The danger is obvious. When financial transactions are made automatically by a cashless, card system, *everything* is set for the fulfillment of Revelation 13:17: "No man might buy or sell, save he that had the mark (card with encoded mark). . . ."

In chapter seven we described the monitoring of all buying and selling by computer when it is combined with monitoring of television viewing habits. The disturbing question then raised by a civil liberties union representative applies here. What if the system becomes mandatory? Please investigate the report we have included and realize that this is as current as today's visit to the grocery store.

What we are seeing is a definite polarization of the spiritual forces of the world. The evil is growing darker, and the good is growing brighter. It is imperative that you make your decision. Now is the time to get out of the world's system and into God's system. Can we change our worldly institutions? Has the media and our educational system gone too far for remedy? Whether the world system can be redeemed or not, we as individuals *can* be. God has given guidelines in His Word for an abundant spirit-filled life *now,* not just in the hereafter.

A young person today is faced with secular humanism in school, mass media manipulation, peer pressure, and direct attack from spiritual influences. You may not be able to take on the entire mass media, but you can teach your children how to move in the power and anointing of the Holy Spirit. They *can* be victorious in overcoming the lies of the enemy. "For we wrestle not against flesh and blood, but against principalities, against powers, against the rulers of the darkness of this world, against spiritual wickedness in high places" (Ephesians 6:12).

Moves change 'stodgy' Sears

By STEVEN GREENHOUSE
N.Y. Times News Service

Sears' new Discover card will offer a wide range of financial services.

AP

CHICAGO — Sears, Roebuck & Co., long viewed as a stodgy giant, is now moving in so many new directions at once that it seems almost dizzying.

On the financial side, the nation's No. 1 retailer will introduce its long-awaited general purpose credit card, Discover, in Atlanta this fall, with nationwide distribution next year. It recently purchased a bank in Delaware and is negotiating to buy another in South Dakota.

And it has installed 306 Sears Financial Network centers — combinations of insurance, securities and real estate brokerage — in its stores. The centers consist of three Sears subsidiaries — an Allstate insurance broker, a Dean Witter securities broker, and a Coldwell Banker real estate broker.

On the retail side, Sears opened a small-scale test store in February in Alma, a central Michigan town of 10,000, and plans to open dozens of such stores throughout small-town America, a new market for the company.

Meanwhile the Chicago-based retailer's 11 new Sears Paint and Hardware Stores in Chicago and New York have done so well that the company plans to open 40 more, all in big cities, next year.

And while all this is going on, Sears is sprucing up many of its 800 existing stores into what it calls Stores of the Future.

"The exciting thing is that Sears is moving," said Edward R. Telling, the 66-year-old chairman of the company once known best for hardware and home appliances. "I know the market is there for what we're doing."

Nevertheless, not all of the new ventures are thriving. Dean Witter, which Sears purchased for $607 million in 1981, lost $35 million last year. But company officials say much of the loss resulted from the brokerage's rapid expansion. It added 1,000 brokers.

. Despite some setbacks in the company's far-reaching expansion, many analysts are enthusiastic about all the changes.

"I think it's all going to pay off in a few years," said John S. Landschulz, an analyst with Mesirow & Co. in Chicago. "Their historic business — retailing — has reached maturity, so they're seeking to invest in dynamic areas to increase their return on investment. Their move into financial services isn't without some risk but it isn't without some experience either."

The basic strategy seems a simple one: to pump more dollars into Sears' vast empire. The more business its stores handle and the more credit billings its computers process, the more profit the company stands to make. Last year the company earned $1.46 billion on $38.83 billion in revenues.

The in-store financial centers are one example of how Sears is trying to milk more business from its existing stores, said Stuart M. Robbins, an analyst with the Donaldson, Lufkin & Jenrette Securities Corp.

"When you're a mature company servicing 80 percent of the population, it's unlikely that you'll attract many new customers," he said, "so you try to get more of the business from the customers you have."

Sears, already strong in durables, is trying to get its customers to spend more on its higher-margin nondurable goods. Thus, the 110 Stores of the Future are increasing the ratio of nondurables such as clothing to durables such as refrigerators.

In addition, Sears, both in its stores and its catalogues, is stressing more fashionable, brand-name clothes instead of the less stylish Sears private labels. Sears also plans to begin selling brand-name electronics, such as Sony and RCA televisions and video cassette recorders, in test markets in San Francisco and Atlanta next month, in addition to its private labels.

Analysts and Sears officials agree that the company's biggest move this year is the introduction of Discover, an orange and black credit card with a sunrise emblazoned on it that will be issued by Sears' own Greenwood Trust Co. Sears already has extensive experience in the credit card field, with 38 million active Sears card holders.

But while the company hopes to build the distribution of the Discover card on its list of existing card holders, the new card will differ markedly from the current one. A customer will be able to use it in restaurants, hotels and stores other than Sears, and will also be able to cash checks, withdraw cash from automated teller machines, and earn interest on money deposited in the card account.

Edward A. Brennan, Sears's president and chief operating officer who will become chairman when Telling retires by the end of the year, said surveys showed that 38 percent of Sears's card holders and 29 percent of non-holders would welcome the Discover card.

Many analysts question, however, whether competing retailers will accept the Discover card. "If it's clear that Sears is associated with the card, it's doubtful that many competing department stores will participate," said Walter F. Loeb, an analyst with Morgan Stanley & Co.

Sears officials responded that the travel and entertainment industry accounts sought by the company have so far responded enthusiastically. As for retailers, Telling said, "If we have millions of cards out, our competitors will be eager to take them because it will help their sales."

Sears officials talk frequently about the "synergies" that their financial network makes possible. Sears hopes that customers who buy a house through Coldwell Banker will obtain property insurance from Allstate, get a mortgage through an arm of the financial network, and use the discount book obtained from Coldwell Banker to buy a Sears washer and dryer.

Appendix II

REASONING FOR THE FAITH AND HOW TO BE
BORN AGAIN

"My people are destroyed for lack of knowl-edge" (Hosea 4:6).

We have been looking at the mechanism for manipulation in the mass media and the results of these actions. Most studies of this subject stop at this point. Our purpose is different. We not only want to reveal how you are being taken advantage of but also how you can be free to be the person God created you to be.

If you are not a Christian, the answer will not work for you. You will not even be able to understand what we will discuss, for "the natural man receiveth not the things of the Spirit of God, for they are foolishness unto him" (1 Corinthians 2:14). If you have been born again and know this for sure, this appendix will be a refresher.

The terms "saved," "born again," "converted,"

etc. have been batted about the last few years by a secular press that has little understanding and even less appreciation for their significance. What does it really mean to be a Christian? No man or woman has the answers in his or her self. One opinion is just as good as another. In ourselves we find only limitation, diversities, and changes. In fact, this deception lies at the heart of the gross error of secularists and humanists. The answer does not rely on man's own ability, his own goodness, his science, his technology, or his potential.

Any honest inquiry into history quickly reveals that man "liberated" from traditional moralities in order to follow his own "potential" is on a road to destruction. When the great civilizations such as Rome turned to self-gratification and self-realization for the basis of their existence, the foundation for their society was shattered. This point cannot be overemphasized. If there are no absolutes or external standards by which to judge our opinions, then there *are* no answers to life.

If we have simply evolved from mindless matter and there is no God, then there are no absolutes and meanings to anything we do. Think about the utter devastation this atheistic philosophy causes. Our law would have absolutely no basis for it's judgments. In fact, why not lie, steal, cheat, murder, and live like animals? If there is no reality behind our morals, who are you to tell me what to do and what not to do? "I'll do my own thing!"

Without a standard of morality our society cannot remain strong. Or worse, our society (state) will become the standard for our behavior (totalitarian/socialistic). As Francis Schaeffer, the renowned Christian philosopher, put it, "When there are no absolutes by which to judge society, then society becomes absolute."[1]

Some people think that the only standard our society needs is a "balance of rights." This is a favorite argument of many so-called intellectuals. It simply states that I should be free to do whatever I want as long as it does not step on someone else's right to do *their* own thing. So, the argument goes, our society does not need an out-of-date book like the Bible telling us what is right and wrong. We simply balance each other's rights and do our own thing.

This seems satisfactory on the surface, but let's take it a step further. Who told you you had rights? Where did these rights come from? Our nation's founding fathers wrote about our "inalienable *God-given* rights;" but if there is no God or ultimate moral standard, where do we assume rights?

Without a standard by which to judge, terms such as "morality" and "rights" become meaningless. We could follow the logic many television shows put out and "learn our lesson from nature." If we were simply more complex animals, that might not be such a bad idea. Unfortunately, however, if we take our lessons from the animal world, the balance of rights theory will surely go down the drain. If there is one lesson nature teaches us, it is that the strong survive, and the weak are eaten. Have you ever seen a lion concerned about the "rights" of its dinner?

The answers we are looking for do not come from *opinion*. We look to a trustworthy source for our reality. To understand how to come into the experience of the abundant Christian life—in fact, to even catch a *glimpse* of it—we must look to the one source that claims to provide the way: the Bible.

The Bible declares that it has the key to eternity and that without Jesus Christ we are "the blind leading the blind" (Matthew 15:14). This fundamental point is so crucial that without a proper appreciation for what the Bible is, what will follow in this book cannot really be understood or applied to your life. With this in mind, I would like to include the following section on Christian apologetics (evidences for faith). I am trying to provide answers to the incredible forces of secular manipulation all around us. If we are to trust the answers put forth in Scripture, we must first be convinced of their validity.

A popular belief is that the Bible has many good things to say but it is not the divine Word of God. If the Bible is not God's Word, then nothing it has to say should be heeded because it would be a misleading lie. The Bible bluntly declares itself to be the Word of God. Second Timothy 3:16 declares, "All scripture is given by inspiration of God, and is profitable for doctrine, for reproof, for correction, for instruction in righteousness." The Bible takes itself so seriously that one of the last verses warns, "If any man shall take away from the words of the book of this prophecy, God shall take away his part out of the book of life" (Revelation 22:19). The Bible, like Jesus, is to be believed totally or rejected. It offers no middle ground.

Some people say Jesus was just a good man. If Jesus was just a good man, then don't listen to a thing He says. Anyone who claims to be the Son of God is either who he says He is, or he is a raving lunatic—certainly not just a good man with wise sayings. Jesus *is* the Son of God, and the Bible is the divinely inspired Word of God. Let's look at a few of the reasons it can be trusted.

Prophecy is the prediction of future events. In Old Testament times, if a man claimed to be a prophet and what he said did not come to pass, he was stoned according to the law. That in itself must have weeded out more than one imposter. One type of prophecy is the prediction of events that were to occur during Biblical times. Later, we will see prophecy as it relates to today.

Would you tend to believe someone who predicted the downfall of America and described exactly to the year when it would regain power? This is exactly what happened during the reign of Nebuchadnezzar of Babylon. Jeremiah predicted Judah would be destroyed and that the Jews would return to restore their nation exactly seventy years later. History records that this happened just as Jeremiah predicted. (See Jeremiah 25:9.)

Another prophet was Isaiah. He predicted that

Bablyon would be defeated and never inhabited again. This must have seemed absurd since Babylon was a world power. Imagine someone predicting Russia would be destroyed and never inhabited again! Yet this is exactly what happened in Babylon's history. Isaiah also predicted the name of the king who would let his people return to Jerusalem and build the temple. King Cyrus proved to be another fulfillment of biblical prophecy.

Perhaps the most dramatic predictions in the Old Testament were in reference to the coming Messiah. Many facts concerning His life and death were predicted hundreds of years before His birth. His crucifixion was described in agonizing detail in Psalm 22. This prophecy is all the more convincing when it is understood that the nation of Israel did not practice crucifixion. This form of execution was introduced hundreds of years later by the Romans.

Other predictions concerning the Messiah included:

SUBJECT	PROPHECY	FULFILLMENT
PLACE OF BIRTH	Micah 5:2	Matthew 2:1
TIME OF BIRTH	Daniel 9:25	Luke 2:1-2
BORN OF A VIRGIN	Isaiah 7:14	Matthew 1:18
MASSACRE OF BABIES	Jeremiah 31:15	Matthew 2:16
BETRAYAL BY JUDAS	Psalm 41:9	Mark 14:10
BETRAYED FOR 30 SILVER PIECES	Zechariah 11:12	Matthew 26:15

BEATEN & SPIT UPON	Isaiah 50:6	Mark 14:65
MOCKED & RIDICULED	Psalm 22:6	Matthew 27:39
BURIAL PLACE	Isaiah 53:9	Matthew 27:57-60
THE RESURRECTION	Psalm 16:10	Matthew 28:9

Many other examples of Biblical prediction have occurred already. Rather than go through extensive revelations, we will hit a few of the more prominent ones.

The Bible predicted the return of the Jews to Israel and the rebirth of that nation (Ezekiel 38:8; 36:24). This happened in 1948. The Bible also predicted that a great enemy would arise to the north of Israel, and it would be in alliance with certain nations (Ezekiel 38:6-15). Russia, a great enemy of Israel, is directly north and is in alliance with predicted nations. Another of Israel's enemies the Word calls "the Kings of the East" is predicted to have an army numbering 200 million. This figure was incredible during Biblical times, but today Red China boasts an army of 200 million! (See Revelation 9:16; 16:12.)

Along with the restoration of Israel and predictions of northern and eastern enemies, the Bible also clearly declares that a ten-nation confederacy will arise with Rome as its headquarters. Today the European Common Market includes ten nations. There is to be a world leader emerging from this confederacy who is called in Revelation the "anti-Christ." He is to head a one-world government that will require all people to receive a mark in order to buy and sell. This mark is predicted to be put on the right hand or the forehead. (See Revelation 13:16.)

Until recently, such ideas seemed open to mockery and contempt. Today, however, the Bible rings as up to date and real as our everyday headlines. Plans are already drawn for one-world government. It already has money printed, computer capabilities for everyone's personal biographical information, and, unfortunately, much support around the globe (including America). The Bible predicted that many people would receive a "mark" in order to buy and sell. As I related before, the Universal Product Code is just such a mark. Incredibly, the code can be broken down as numerically encoded 666.[2] Once again the Bible proves its trustworthiness.

Now that you have seen the absolute accuracy of biblical prophecy, you should know the next great event on the calendar: the return of Jesus Christ. If all the predictions so far have come true, doesn't it stand to reason that the few remaining events will occur just as the other 98 percent have done? The Bible is true. It stands up to honest investigation.

Before we move on, a few more points should be mentioned regarding the intellectual handiwork of God. A growing group of scientists declare that scientific evidence clearly demonstrates the earth was created. The Institute for Creation Research[3] and the Bible Science Association[4] are two organizations working to see that scientific creation is given its proper place in our educational system. They point out one of the many basic flaws in evolution. The Law of Thermodynamics indicates that complex organisms tend to break *down*, not build up. It looks very much like our universe is winding down, not evolving into a higher order.

Evolution is based on just the opposite assumption. In essence, evolutionists assume that elements left to themselves will evolve into higher, more complex organisms. The whole theory asks a giant step of faith: gas, if left to itself long enough, will eventually evolve into a man!

More evidence for the Christian faith involves the lives of the apostles. This is a very interesting factor since it relates to the resurrection of Jesus. History records (as well as the Bible) that the disciples were scattered and terrified after Jesus was taken and crucified. Although the followers of Jesus were initially frightened of their circumstances, *something* happened to turn those fearful doubters into bold, vibrant witnesses for the Lord. In fact, the transformation was so complete that they were even willing to die for their witness.

The one event each disciple declared to be the deciding factor in their lives was the resurrection of Jesus. Each man said he had seen the Lord after His death. If the disciples had not seen the risen Lord, would they have died for a lie? All that the authorities would have wanted was a denouncement of the witness of the resurrection. It would have been easy for the believers simply to say it was a hoax or to deliver the body of Jesus they had stolen from the grave.

Yet this is not what happened. These men gave their lives for the firm belief that they had seen Jesus after He rose from the grave. Many men in history have given their lives for lies (Kamakazee pilots), yet they actually believed they were in the truth. If the disciples of Jesus died for a lie, they were of all men most foolish—they would have died for a lie, *knowing* it was a lie.

One of the most convincing aspects of Christian apologetics involves a look into present-day experiences in the supernatural realm. Literally millions of people have testified to unusual incidents that cannot be explained by natural means. We will only look at a few well-documented or personally experienced cases.

Evidence Of A Spirit-World

A remarkable incident occurred in Manilla, Philippines involving Dr. Lester Sumrall. While working to found a new church, he heard a radio report of a young woman in a local prison who was apparently being tormented by a horrible demon. The press called it ''the thing.''[5] Top governmental officials and newsmen were covering the story. It was getting front page coverage. This possessed girl had said two men would die, and they did die within a very short time. Strange manifestations occurred in the cell as the young lady was thrown about, choked, and even bitten by this unseen tormentor. These events were witnessed by dozens of observers and are documented in medical and prison records.

When Dr. Sumrall finally was allowed to visit the cell, he instantly recognized the source of this unseen power. The answer did not lie in psychology or even in medical treatment. There were demon powers inside the girl that had to be faced and overcome in the power of Jesus' name. After a glorious victory in which the girl was completely set free, the headlines read: "DEVIL LOSES ROUND ONE." The reporters did not understand that the fight had been won. Satan was down for the count.

I came personally face to face with demon possession while working for a television ministry in South Carolina. One night a wild-eyed woman walked into our studio demanding to see Joanne Thompson, a lady with extensive experience in the deliverance ministry. Since Joanne had gone home for the evening, we tried to minister to the woman but met with little success. We finally had to call Joanne back in.

When Joanne came in the door, she instantly recognized the presence of evil spirits in the woman. While we had tried to deal with the problem relying mainly on our own understanding, she ministered in the supernatural realm of the spirit. One of the first things she told the troubled lady was to hand over her gun! The rest of us almost fell over. How did Joanne know the lady was carrying a concealed gun? While at first denying she had a gun, at Joanne's persistence, the lady finally handed over a small pistol. She was planning to kill someone that very night. Then Joanne discerned through the gifts of the Holy Spirit that the woman was also concealing a knife. Sure enough, it wasn't long before the lady was handing over a knife.

Evil spirits had bound this woman so completely that she couldn't even say the name of Jesus. Joanne took authority over the spirits and cast them out one by one. Before leaving that night, the woman who could not even repeat "Jesus" was raising her hands and praising Him with a new-found freedom. We were given eyewitness proof of the futility of trying this ministry in the power of the flesh. The supernatural power of God must be flowing through your life before these results will be evident.

Another example involves a family in the town where we now live. A familiar spirit occupies their home. Objects move mysteriously, cabinets open, footsteps can be heard walking across the floor, and many strange events such as voices coming from empty rooms have become part of their normal routine. This family witnesses the spirit-world continually but will not take the necessary steps to receive the Lord. They have become comfortable with this familiar spirit, not knowing that the real intention of the demon is to destroy them.

I personally witnessed this phenomenon in another house in Jacksonville, Florida. A confirmed unbeliever in demons when entering, I left the next morning convinced. No one on earth could make me believe there wasn't "something else out there."

Many people are coming out of the occult today and witnessing to an underground satanic worship few of us have even dared to believe. Witchcraft is rampant in this country. Many former witches have come forward to reveal widespread activity in the dark side of the supernatural. In her book, *Escape From Witchcraft*, Roberta Blankenship describes how she was drawn into the occult after conducting a successful seance. At the time, she was only in the sixth grade.[6]

In addition to the supernatural experiences and logical evidences to support the truth of the Bible, the most important proof is you. There is something in all of us that declares the existence of a Creator. Deep in your heart you know what I am saying is true. *You* are the best evidence for biblical reality.

How To Be Born Again

Once a belief in the authority of the Bible is settled, the next step is to do what the Bible says to do. Specific instructions in the Word of God show us how to understand the battle that can undermine our families and our nation. These are guidelines not only to understanding but to victory.

The secular humanist declares that man must look to himself—and himself alone—for the answers to the problems facing our world. The humanist sees traditional theistic religion as a threat. In contrast, the Bible says man should not—and cannot—find the answers in himself. The very nature of man and the universe is in dispute here: a very fundamental difference lies in the views of reality presented. If you believe the Bible, and there are very good reasons to believe it, the answers to life lie within its pages.

To begin, the Bible says man was created in the image of God (not that man created God in his image). God, a Spirit, touched flesh from dust and created a living soul. (See Genesis 2:7.) Man was created as spirit, soul, and body. (See 1 Thessalonians 5:23.) Just as the triune God was Spirit, so man was created spiritually alive and in touch with God. Only one restriction was put on man: He should be obedient and not eat one particular type of food. God promised that the day man disobeyed in rebellion he would surely die.

Man did disobey, and he did die that very day as God had warned; but, as most of us know, Adam did not die physically that day. He went on to father many children and lived a long life on earth. Adam's soul (mind, personality) did not die, for in all appearances he was the same man as before— eating, talking, laughing, hoping, etc.

What died that day was the spiritual side of man. The connection was broken with God. Those who worship God "must worship Him in Spirit" (John 4:24). This basic foundational doctrine of Christianity forever separates the humanist, atheist, communist, and secularist from a true Christian. This is the truth of the basic sinful nature of man—every man is born in sin and needs a savior. (See Romans 5:12-7:14.)

We are not basically good and only learn evil from our society. We do not have to teach children to be selfish. We have to teach them to share and not to be selfish. Unless this basic teaching of the Bible can be accepted, there is no need to go any further. If we have no need of a savior, then Jesus died in vain and was merely a sadly deluded dreamer.

Because man *does* need a savior, as the Bible teaches, Jesus had to die for our sins. Contrary to the mistaken teachings of humanism, man cannot redeem himself. Every sin ever committed will be paid for. God is a just God, and, according to His own law, sin must be accounted for. (See Romans 6:23.) No sin is ever just forgiven and forgotten. *Someone* is going to have to pay for it. Fortunately, God's love was so great for us that He gave His only Son to suffer and die on the cross for *our* sins. Jesus took our sins on Himself. Someone did pay for every sin you and I have ever committed (or ever will). Jesus paid it all. All we have to do is receive His loving gift of life.

Our next step, therefore, in understanding how to safeguard our families and combat the manipulation that tries to drag them down is to become alive spiritually. As Jesus put it, we "must be born again" (John 3:3,7). This step is essential if we are

141

to truly understand the world around us. Without this new birth, we are "blind leaders of the blind" (Matthew 15:14).

To experience the birth of your spirit and become a "new creation" (2 Corinthians 5:17), you must simply put your life into the hands of Jesus. It is sort of an exchange—your sinful life for His spotless, beautiful, and abundant life. We must repent of our sins, surrender our lives to Jesus, and receive Him into our hearts with simple childlike faith. This one act of faith, this one turning to God, sparks in us the very life of heaven. If you have never done so, right now give your life to Jesus and receive Him as your Lord and Savior. He loves you!

Appendix III

CHRISTIAN ORGANIZATION AND RESOURCE GUIDE

Music/Backmasking

* Bob Larson, *Rock, For Those Who Listen To The Words And Don't Like What They Hear* (Tyndale House, 1980).

* Marty Tingelhoff, *Living Word* (P.O. Box 886 Kingsport, TN 37662).

* Peters and Merrill, *Rocks Hidden Persuaders: The Truth About Backmasking* (Bethany House, 1985).

NEA, Humanism, Social Agenda

* Samuel Blemenfeld, *NEA, Trojan Horse In American Education* (Paradigm, 1984).

* James Hitchcock, *What Is Secular Humanism?* (Servant Books, 1982).

* Tim LaHaye, *The Hidden Censors* (Fleming Revell, 1984).

* William A. Stanmeyer, *Clear And Present Danger* (Servant Books, 1983).

* Francis and Franky Schaeffer, Various books, articles, and films, including *A Christian Manifesto* (Crossway Books, 1981) and *Bad News For Modern Man* (Crossway Books, 1984).

* Don Wildemon, *National Federation For Decency* (P.O. Drawer 2440 Tupelo, MS 38803).

New Age Movement, One World Government, One-World Finances

* Constance Cumbey, *The Hidden Dangers Of The Rainbow* (Huntington House, 1983).

* Mary Stewart Relfe, *The New Money System* and *When Your Money System Fails* (Ministries, Inc. P.O. Box 4038 Montgomery, AL 36104).

* William Bowen, *Globalism: America's Demise* (Huntington House, 1983).

Occult-Demonology

* Joanne Thompson (Box 1616 Greenville, SC 29602).

* Irene Park, *The Witch That Switched* (P.O. Box 1394 New Port Richey, FL 34291).

* Mike Warnke, *The Satan Seller* (Logos, 1972).

Pornography, Abortion

* National Right to Life (Suite 402, 419 7th Street NW Washington, DC 20004).
* Chris Schlabach, *Come Alive Ministries* (P.O. Box 882 Hartville, OH 44632).
* *Citizens for Decency through Law, Inc.* (2331 West Royal Palm Road, Suite 105 Phoenix, Arizona 85021).
* William A. Stanmeyer, *The Seduction Of Society* (Servant Books, 1984).

Biblical Science, Creationism

* *Institute for Creation Research* (Midwest Center 1319 Brush Circle Naperville, IL 60540).
* *Bible-Science Association, Inc.* (6245 Newton Ave. S. Richfield, MN 55423).

NOTES

Chapter 2

1. Joe Saltzman, "The Legacy of *M*A*S*H,"* *USA Today* (July 1983): p. 61.
2. Tim LaHaye, *The Hidden Censors* (New Jersey: Fleming H. Revell, 1984), p. 132.
3. "Whose Ox?" *Forbes Magazine* (September 15, 1985): p. 110.
4. Constance Cumbey, *The Hidden Dangers Of The Rainbow* (Shreveport: Huntington House, 1983), p. 194.
5. Rose K. Goldsen, *The Show And Tell Machine* (New York: Dial Press, 1974), pp. 164, 174, 176.
6. Joan Ganz Cooney, *USA Today* (September 1984): p. 85.
7. Goldsen, p. 2.
8. Cooney, p. 85.

9. Michael Satchell, "Does Hollywood Sell Drugs To Kids?" *Parade* (July 21, 1985): p. 4.
10. *N.F.D. Journal,* (March 1985; May/June 1985), National Federation for Decency.
11. S. Robert Lichter and Stanley Rothman, "Media And Business Elites," *Public Opinion* (October/November 1981): p. 42.

Chapter 3

1. Lichter, p. 42.
2. Ibid., p. 45.
3. Ibid.
4. Ibid., p. 44.
5. Maura Clancey and Michael J. Robinson, "General Election Coverage: Part 1," *Public Opinion* (December/January 1985): p. 49.
6. Ibid.
7. Ibid., p. 50.
8. Lichter, p. 60.
9. Ibid.

Chapter 4

1. Martin Seiden, *Who Controls The Mass Media?* (New York: Basic Books, 1974), p. 174.
2. Wilson Brian Key, *Subliminal Seduction* (New York: Prentice-Hall, 1974), p. 79.

3. Kim Foltz, "Ads Popping Up All Over," *Newsweek* (August 12, 1985): p. 50.

4. Goldsen, p. 6.

5. Key, p. 78.

6. Vance Packard, *Hidden Persuaders* (New York: Washington Square Press, 1957), p. 269.

7. Ibid., pp. 269-270.

8. Goldsen, p. 392. (Also see Packard, p. 255.)

9. Foltz, p. 50. (Also see Packard, pp. 5, 207.)

10. Seiden, p. 183.

11. Packard, p. 12.

12. Key, p. 94.

13. Ibid. (Pictorial section.)

14. "The Bum's Rush In Advertising," *Time* (December 1, 1980): p. 95.

15. Mark Crispin, "Getting Dirty," *New Republic* (June 2, 1982): p. 25. (Key pictorial section.)

16. Furvashi and McCarthy, *Social Issues Of Marketing In The American Economy* (Ohio: Grid, Inc., 1971), p. 68.

17. Seiden, p. 174.

18. Bishop and Hubbard, *Let The Seller Beware* (Washington: National Press, 1969), p. 150.

19. Seiden, p. 182. (Also see Packard, p. 267.)

20. Seiden, p. 175.

Chapter 5

1. James Hitchcock, *What Is Secular Humanism?* (Michigan: Servant Books, 1982), p. 81.
2. Goldsen, p. 10.
3. Ibid., p. 273.
4. Altschuler and Regush, *Open Reality* (New York: Putnuam, 1974), p. 95.
5. Ibid., p. 83.
6. Mary Gardiner Jones, "The Cultural And Social Impact Of Advertising On American Society," *Consumerism, Search For Consumer Interest* (Aaker and Day, New York Free Press), p. 430.
7. Packard, p. 6.
8. Altschuler, p. 84.
9. Packard, p. 260.
10. Key, p. 83.
11. Ernest Dichter, *Handbook Of Consumer Motivations* (New York: McGraw-Hill, 1964), pp. 87, 423.
12. Ibid., p. 66.
13. Ibid., p. 81.
14. Ibid., p. 473.

Chapter 6

1. "TV Networks: Centers Of News Power," *US News And World Report* (August 15, 1977): p. 31.

2. "Are The TV Networks Selling Too Many Ads?" *Business Week* (September 18, 1978): p. 26.

3. David Pauly, "Big Media, Big Money," *Newsweek* (April 1, 1985): p. 52.

4. Sharon Nelton, "More Slices In A Bigger Pie," *Nations Business* (January 1985): p. 64.

5. Alvin P. Sanoff, "TV News Growing Too Powerful?" *US News And World Report* (June 9, 1980): p. 60.

6. Pauly, p. 59. Also see *US News* (August 15, 1977): p. 31.

Chapter 7

1. Joshua Meyrowitz, "The 19-inch Neighborhood," *Newsweek* (July 22, 1985): p. 8.

2. Alvin P. Sanoff, "America's Press," *US News & World Report* (August 15, 1977): p. 31.

3. William Rivers, "The News Media: The Other Government," *USA Today* (July 1983): p. 59.

4. Goldsen, p. 144.

5. Sanoff (June 9, 1980): p. 59. (Also see Meyrowitz, p. 8.)

6. "Power Of Media Elite," *Intellect* (July 1977): p. 10.

7. Rivers, p. 59.

8. Packard, pp. 7, 166.

9. Joseph Poindexter, "Shaping the Consumer," *Psychology Today* (May 1983): p. 64.

10. Ibid.
11. *Intellect* (July 1977): p. 10. (Also see Lichter, p. 42.)
12. Dichter, pp. 6, 459, 420.

Chapter 8

1. Goldsen, p. 120.
2. David A. Aaker and George S. Day, *Consumerism—Search For The Consumer Interest* (New York: Free Press, 1971) p. 430.
3. Robert B. Choate and Nancy DeBevoise, "How To Make Trouble," *MS. Magazine* (April 1975): p. 91.
4. Barbara Ehrenreich and David Nasaw, "Kids As Consumers And Commodities," *The Nation* (May 14, 1983): pp. 597-599.
5. Ibid., p. 597.
6. Bever, Smith, Bensen, and Johnson, "Young-viewer's Troubling Response To TV Ads," *Harvard Business Review* (November/December 1975): p. 109.
7. Stephen Clint, "TV As Behavior Model," American Education (July 1975): p. 40.
8. J.W. Stein, "Shotgun Wedding: Television and the Schools," *USA Today* (November 1983): p. 431.
9. Ron Goulart, *The Assault On Childhood* (Los Angeles: Sherbourne Press, 1969), p. 129.

10. Marie Winn, "The Plug-in Drug," *Saturday Evening Post* (November 1977): pp. 40, 41.

11. Hugh Furhasha and Jerome McCarthy, *Social Issues Of Marketing In The American Economy* (Grid, Inc.: 1971), pp. 73,74.

12. Elizabeth Roberts, "Television and Sexual Learning in Childhood," *Television And Behavior,* vol. 2 (National Institute Of Mental Health: Rockville, Maryland), pp. 209-210, 220-222.

13. Ibid., p. 217.

14. William F. Fore, "Mass Media's Mythic World: At Odds With Christian Values," *Christian Century* (January 19, 1977): p. 34.

15. "Warning From Washington," *Time* (May 17, 1982): p. 34.

16. Stein, p. 57.

17. Ibid.

18. Goldsen, p. 287.

19. Key, pp. 67, 68.

Chapter 9

1. Key, p. 67.

2. Goldsen, p.

3. John Caughey, "Fantasy Friends Fill A Gap In People's Lives," *US News and World Report* (July 16, 1984): p. 106.

4. Fore, p. 33.

5. Joe Salzman, "The Seductive Picture Show," *USA Today* (September 1982): p. 59.

6. Roberts, pp. 209, 210.
7. Joe Salzman, "Television's Dilemma: Information vs. Entertainment," *USA Today* (January 1984): pp. 92, 93.
8. Key, p. 67.
9. Dorothy Cohen, "Television and the Perception of Reality," *Education Digest* (March 1977): p. 12. (Also see Fore, p. 33.)
10. Fore, p. 33.
11. Gerbner, Morgan, Signorielli, "Programming Health Portrayals: What Viewers See, Say, and Do," *The Annenberg School Of Communication, University Of Pennsylvania*, from *Television and Behavior, vol. 2.,* The National Institute Of Mental Health.
12. Fore, p. 33.
13. Cohen, p. 10.
14. Joe Salzman, "This Is the Way the World Ends—CLICK," *USA Today* (September 1983): p. 33.

Chapter 10

1. Packard, p. 160.
2. David Hapgood, *The Screwing Of The Average Man* (New York: Doubleday, 1974), p. 180.
3. David Sanford, *Who Put The Con In Consumer?* (New York: Liverright, 1972), p. 119.
4. Hapgood, p. 175.
5. Ibid., pp. 194, 199.

Chapter 11

1. Marty Tingelhoff, "Expose of Rock, Soul, and Country Music," *Living Word* (P.O. Box 886, Kingsport, Tennessee 37662) Tape 1, Side 1 of a 4 part cassette tape series.
2. Peters and Merrill, *Rock's Hidden Persuaders: The Truth About Backmasking* (Minneapolis, Bethany House, 1985), p. 78.
3. Bob Larson, *Rock, For Those Who Listen To The Words And Don't Like What They Hear* (Illinois: Tyndale House, 1980), pp. 41, 44, 126.
4. Ibid, p. 41.
5. Ibid., pp. 43, 146.
6. Tingelhoff, Tape 1, Side 1. (Cassette tape series.)

Chapter 12

1. Waters, Kasindorf, Huch, Copeland, Wilson, "TV Comedy: What It's Teaching The Kids," *Newsweek* (May 7, 1979): p. 64.
2. Goldsen, p. 72.
3. Susan Witty, "The Laugh-makers," *Psychology Today* (August 1983): p. 24.
4. Richard Dale, "Fun, As In Funeral," *Science Digest* (March 1972): p. 7.
5. Ibid., pp. 72, 73.
6. Waters, p. 67, 68.

7. Dale, p. 69, 72.
8. Witty, p. 26.

Chapter 13

1. Richard Ferrell, "Demons, Saviours, and Spiritual Warfare: Religion's Image In Current Films," *USA Today* (January 1984): p. 89.
2. Bob Thomas, "Realism Is Out, Escapism In," *AP Wire Report* (August 15, 1985).
3. Ibid.
4. Ferrell, p. 90.
5. Ibid.
6. Todd McCarthy, "Sand Castles," *Film Comment* (March/April 1982): p. 55.

Chapter 14

1. Packard, pp. 243, 250.
2. Dichter, pp. 420, 459.

Appendix I

1. Constance Cumbey, *Hidden Dangers Of The Rainbow* (Shreveport: Huntington House 1983,) p. 20.

2. Irene Park, *The Witch That Switched* (Irene Park Ministries P.O. Box 1394 New Port Richey, FL 34291).

3. Samuel Blumenfeld NEA, *Trojan Horse In American Education* (Paradigm 1984), p. 177.

4. James Hitchcock, *What Is Secular Humanism?* (Ann Arbor: Servant Books 1982), p. 11.

5. Mary Stewart Relfe, *The New Money System* and *When Your Money System Fails* (Ministries, Inc. PO Box 4038 Montgomery, AL 36104), p. 32.

Appendix II

1. Francis A. Schaeffer.

2. Relfe, *The New Money System* (Box 4038 Montgomery, AL).

3. Institute for Creation Research—Midwest Center (1319 Brush Hill Circle Naperville, IL 60540).

4. Bible-Science Association, Inc. (6245 Newton Avenue S. Richfield, MN 55423).

5. Lester Sumrall, *Bitten By Devils* (LeSEA PO Box 12 South Bend, IN 46624).

6. Roberta Blankenship, *Escape From Witchcraft* (Grand Rapids: Zondervan 1972).